LAST CALL at the OASIS

a participant° guide
MEDIA

LAST CALL at the OASIS

The Global Water Crisis and Where We Go From Here

edited by **Karl Weber**

PublicAffairs
New York

Excerpt from *The Day New York Went Dry* by Charles Einstein is reprinted by permission of the author's estate.

PublicAffairs books are available at special discounts for bulk purchases in the US by corporations, institutions, and other organizations. For more information, please contact the Special Markets Department at the Perseus Books Group, 2300 Chestnut Street, Suite 200, Philadelphia, PA 19103, call (800) 810-4145, ext. 5000, or e-mail special.markets@perseusbooks.com.

Book Design by Pauline Brown

Library of Congress Cataloging-in-Publication Data

Last call at the oasis : the global water crisis and where we go from here / edited by Karl Weber. — 1st ed.
 p. cm. — (A participant media guide)
Includes index.
ISBN 978-1-58648-978-6 (pbk. original) — ISBN 978-1-61039-144-3 (electronic)
1. Water-supply—Management. 2. Water-supply—International cooperation. 3. Water conservation. I. Weber, Karl, 1953-
TD313.5.L37 2012
333.91—dc23
                                                            2011051868
First Edition

10 9 8 7 6 5 4 3 2 1

CONTENTS

Part III | GETTING INVOLVED: RESOURCES FOR LEARNING AND ACTIVISM

PREFACE

The headlines tell the story: "Water Pollution Report Sends Shockwaves Through Shale Gas Industry"; "In China City of Four Million, No Water"; "Radioactive Water Spills at New Brunswick Nuclear Plant"; "Environmentalists Oppose Proposed Wyoming-to-Colorado Water Pipeline"; "Water Is More Important Than Oil for UAE: Mohammed bin Zayed"; "Water Risk to 500 Australian Farms, Dairy Industry Fears"; "New Reports Finds Aging Water Infrastructure Burdens US Economy"; "Spread of Fracking Leads to Fears of Water Shortages." That's literally *one day's* harvest of water-related stories from Google News—and we stopped listing them because we got tired, not because we reached the end of the collection.

Water woes are everywhere, and in a host of forms: floods and droughts, shortages of potable water, pollution and contamination, overuse and misuse in developed countries, lack of access in developing countries, crumbling infrastructure, endangered water habitats, excessive and ecologically dangerous damming, political and military battles over water rights . . . the list goes on and on. This poses the question: How have we humans allowed ourselves to reach such a crisis point with one of the most vital necessities of life (second only to the air we breathe)?

That's the question that the important new documentary film *Last Call at the Oasis* sets out to explore—and the same question we tackle in this book.

If you've seen the movie, you've probably picked up this companion book in hopes of learning more about the complex issues so vividly depicted by filmmaker Jessica Yu. If you haven't seen the movie, we strongly recommend it—and we hope you'll also read this book to enjoy a deeper, wider-ranging exploration of many of the crucial water challenges our planet faces today.

Here's an overview of the book's contents.

After a brief prologue, "All Bets Are Off," which sets the stage through an excerpt from a prescient novel about a devastating water shortage in New York City—originally published almost fifty years ago!—Part One offers several perspectives on the worsening water crises the peoples of the world face. "Water Realities" presents a summary of key facts, statistics, trends, and relationships, painting a stark picture of our reliance on dwindling, endangered water supplies and the challenges we'll face in remedying the problem. In "Exploring Oasis," director Jessica Yu describes the experience of researching and filming *Last Call at the Oasis,* and what she learned about the psychology of water use—and water abuse—in the process.

Next, heroic pollution fighter Lynn Henning tells her own story in "From Farmer to Water Activist," explaining how industrial farming is threatening an age-old way of life in America's Midwest—as well as the water supplies on which we all rely. In "Clean Water—The Price of Gold?" hydrogeologist Robert Moran reveals how "resource extraction" industries such as energy and mining are damaging water supplies worldwide, and often doing so in near-total secrecy created by uncontrolled corporate power. Finally Alex Prud'homme, author of the book *The Ripple Effect,* which helped inspire *Last Call at the Oasis,* recounts his own education in the realities of the world's water, and warns us that, as the title of his chapter states, there's "No Time to Waste."

In Part Two of the book, we shift from reviewing the problems with water to describing possible solutions. First, today's leading expert on water and the environment, Peter H. Gleick of the Pacific Institute, explains his famous concept of the "soft path"—a more sustainable approach to improving global water supply than traditional massive infrastructure projects—in his chapter "A Way Forward?" Then Gary White, CEO of Water.org, explains in "In Our Lifetime" how creative ways of thinking about, organizing, funding, and managing water projects can bring essential water resources for the first time to the billions of people in the developing world. In their chapter, "Drawing Water," visionary designers Hadley Arnold and Peter Arnold describe their new approach to urban planning, which is already beginning to transform how western cities, such as Burbank, California, handle their precious water resources. And in her chapter, "From Crisis to Competitive Advantage," Robyn Beavers explains how farseeing companies, such as Google, are recognizing the importance of sustainable water management and altering their resource-use policies accordingly.

Next, in "Diamonds in Disguise," legal expert and acclaimed author Robert Glennon discusses the market and regulatory failures that underlie today's water crises, and explains how redesigned systems for organizing the distribution and use of water can encourage conservation and ensure that all people have enough water for their needs. Two chapters of highly practical advice come next. In "Ten Simple Ways You Can Help Protect Our Water," the National Resources Defense Council offers ideas everyone can begin following today to reduce pollution and end needless water waste. And in "Nine Ecofabulous Ways to Save Water at Home—And Do It with Style," Zem Joaquin offers tips for smarter ways of using water in your bathroom, kitchen, and elsewhere at home, including recommendations of new products and technologies that are making sustainable living not just practical but fun.

Finally, in "Endless Resourcefulness," William McDonough, perhaps today's most acclaimed thinker about the relationship between humans and the planet they inhabit, offers a series of provocative, fascinating observations about the value of water and the power of intelligent design to enhance and expand that value. McDonough's insights conclude Part Two on an optimistic note: water, he says, is a potentially infinite resource—providing we have the wisdom and the will to use it correctly.

The last section of the book, Part Three, is a resource guide containing five annotated lists that readers wanting to get further involved in water issues will find useful. Included are a list of water-related organizations that deserve your support, lists of online information tools and activist campaigns you'll find illuminating and inspiring, an annotated list of some of the best books about water and the global challenges we face in managing and conserving it, and finally, a hat-tip to the people who brought *Last Call at the Oasis* to a theater near you.

In the course of editing this book and working with the brilliant, committed authors who've contributed to it, I've come to learn how complex, fascinating, and important are the water issues our species is grappling with. No single book could hope to capture every nuance of these issues. But I hope you'll find *Last Call at the Oasis*— this book as well as the film of the same name—to be a valuable introduction to the challenges of water and a small but meaningful step toward discovering a more sustainable, water-friendly way of life for you, your family, and the larger human community.

Karl Weber
Irvington, New York
December 2011

PROLOGUE: "ALL BETS ARE OFF"

An Excerpt from The Day New York Went Dry by Charles Einstein (1964)

Journalist, novelist, and screenwriter Charles Einstein (1926–2007) enjoyed a long and varied career working on both coasts of the United States. Today he probably is best remembered for his writing about baseball, particularly his coverage of the career of San Francisco Giants star Willie Mays for that city's *Chronicle* and *Examiner* newspapers, and for his editing of a much-loved series of *Fireside Books of Baseball*. But Einstein was also a successful writer of fiction. His novel T*he Bloody Spur* was made into the 1956 film noir classic *While the City Sleeps* by director Fritz Lang.

Einstein's 1964 novel, *The Day New York Went Dry,* from which this excerpt is taken, offers a prescient glimpse of a world in which supplies of freshwater are running out—with catastrophic consequences for modern society. In the excerpt, Einstein's protagonist, reporter Don Marlowe, is trying to convince a skeptical group of policy makers that a drought and water shortage plaguing New York City represents more than just a temporary inconvenience, but rather the opening assault from what could prove to be an existential threat to the city and its 8 million residents.

Marlowe knew now he was getting through to them. For the first time, he reached into the pocket of his suit coat, drew out a small folded square of paper, unfolded it, and gazed down at the notes he had made.

"Realistically," he said, "there are five possibilities. The first one is that it rains like hell. That'll take care of our problem right there. I mean rain rain rain. And it looks like this just isn't going to happen.

"Number two—the city can cut off the water a certain number of hours per day. I mean just plain cut it off. Serve places like hospitals with tank trucks if necessary, but for x number of hours a day just stop the delivery of water."

A voice said: "What's wrong with that?"

"What's wrong with that," Marlowe said, "is not when you stop it but where you stop it. And what do people do when it's stopped? Do they use toilets? Do they wash clothes? Does the brewery in Long Island City make beer? Can the fire department fight fires?" His voice dropped. "Worst of all, what is there to keep people from hoarding water while it's turned on, against the time when it's off? Oh . . ." he nodded ". . . you can do it. It takes what amounts to a police state, but you can do it. I wouldn't recommend it."

Again he nodded. "Number three, you can tap new sources. The Hudson's there." He paused imperceptibly. "The Delaware's there. But you have to look at your equipment. There are places right now, up the Hudson, where, emergency pipes lead to the river, in case delivery from farther upstate is interrupted. But those pipes are for that purpose. They don't contemplate drought. If the river's down, then the pipes have to be lowered some way to get into it. And then you have an added purification problem. We're not set up to tap river water."

Again he nodded. "Number four, we can figure out a way to take what's already been done and literally talk the people into conserving water. I take it that this is what this meeting's for. I don't mean not sprinkling or not shaving or not washing cars or not cleaning streets. That's already been done. I mean a totally new, additional approach to the entire problem. Gentlemen, more than fifty percent of our water usage is straight residential. These are the people who read the papers and the signs and the television commercials. And that's what I suggest here. I don't know what else this meeting is for."

A voice at the table: "Those are the four possibilities?" Marlowe gazed at his notes. "Just about. Actually, there are five."

"What's the fifth?"

"That we get less than normal rainfall."

"Then what?"

"Then all bets are off."

Part I | THE COMING WATER CRISIS

I

WATER REALITIES

By the Editor[1]

Water: It's essential to life on Earth . . . a vital medium for the nutrients that sustain us . . . a feature in the landscapes most beloved by humans everywhere . . . and in all its forms, from raindrops to rivers to waterfalls to fountains to clouds, ice, and snow, perhaps the most varied and beautiful substance on our planet. When our bodies run short of water, during strenuous exercise or in the dog days of summer, we crave it intensely and imbibe it with unalloyed delight; when water is scarce, societies will pay almost any price to obtain it, building giant dams and reservoirs, aqueducts and pipelines, purification plants and desalination systems, to secure the precious fluid. Yet when water seems plentiful, we take it for granted. And so most of us in the developed nations of the world give little thought, day in and day out, to the water we rely upon.

Hence this chapter, whose purpose is to ground our conversations about water in some of the challenging realities we so casually ignore.

---

1 Thanks to Sylvia Lee (manager, water) at the Skoll Global Threats Fund and to Sarah Newman (researcher, social action) at Participant Media for providing much of the information contained in this chapter.

QUANTITY: HOW MUCH WATER DO WE HAVE?
HOW MUCH DO WE NEED?

Water comes in three forms—gas, solid, and liquid—which routinely transmute into one another through the processes of freezing, thawing, evaporation, and condensation. These three forms of water, in finite amounts, continue to be recycled through Earth's global ecosystem in the ever-renewing hydrological cycle. This means we are drinking the same water that the dinosaurs drank, that Cleopatra bathed in, and that splashed in the gardens of Versailles during the reign of Louis XIV. We can't create water; the volume of water on our planet is fixed and somehow must support all human, animal, and plant life for as long as we dwell on the earth.

Though 70 percent of Earth's surface is covered by water, less than 1 percent of that water is the freshwater essential for our survival. With the human population on our planet having surpassed the 7 billion mark, it's no wonder we are living in an era of increased water scarcity and variability. An estimated 1 billion people lack access to safe drinking water, while 2 billion lack adequate sanitation.[2]

According to Jay Famiglietti, professor at the University of California at Irvine and director of the UC Center for Hydrologic Modeling, "Our work is showing that virtually all of the aquifers in the mid-latitudes (these are the arid and semiarid regions of the world) are under threat and have been losing water for many years."[3] A study in *Nature* found that 3.4 billion people live in regions where their freshwater supply is insecure.[4]

---

2 Wendy DeWolf, "Engineering Clean Water," *Yale Scientific Magazine*, April 3, 2011, www.yalescientific.org/2011/04/engineering-clean-water, accessed May 11, 2011.
3 E-mail, Jay Famiglietti, May 11, 2011.
4 "Water Map Shows Billions at Risk of 'Water Insecurity,'" BBC News, www.bbc.co.uk/news/science-environment-11435522, accessed May 12, 2011.

According to other analyses, one-third of the global population lives in "water-stressed" areas and 8 percent in "severely water-stressed" regions, which includes parts of the western United States, along with places such as Australia, southern Africa, and northern Mexico.[5] Depending on the region, "water stress" has different meanings. In developed areas, such as the American Southwest, "water stress" refers to the region's inability to support further economic development because of water shortages. In developing countries, the term means inadequate water for drinking, sanitation, and agriculture, while in emerging economies (such as China and India), it means the growing middle class's lifestyle needs cannot be met.

Several factors contribute to these growing water stresses, including population growth (global population is expected to hit 10 billion by 2050),[6] dwindling water supplies, climate change, water mismanagement, and economic development (since most forms of manufacturing, energy production, and resource extraction use large amounts of water).

In the United States, drinking water comes from massive, intricate systems comprising rivers, streams, lakes, wetlands, aquifers (natural underground water reservoirs), and other bodies of water. Three major river systems—the Colorado, the Rio Grande, and the San Joaquin—provide water to eight states. The largest aquifer in the United States is the Ogallala, stretching across seven states, from North Dakota to Texas. Forests, meadows, and other open spaces are critical to capturing water for these systems. In fact, an estimated

5 DeWolf, "Engineering Clean Water"; Patricia Gober, "Global Warming Aside, Fresh Water Dwindling," *Arizona Republic,* August 17, 2008, www.azcentral.com/arizonarepublic/viewpoints/articles/2008/08/17/20080817vip-gober0817.html, accessed May 11, 2011.

6 Justin Gillis and Celia W. Duggar, "Coming to a Planet Near You: 3 Billion More Mouths to Feed," *Green* (blog), *New York Times,* May 4, 2011, http://green.blogs.nytimes.com/2011/05/04/coming-to-a-planet-near-you-3-billion-more-mouths-to-feed/?scp=1&sq=2050%20overpopulation&st=cse, accessed May 11, 2011.

18 percent of the nation's total water supply and 60 percent of the water used in the western states comes from National Forests managed by the US Department of Agriculture.[7]

These natural sources of water are converted for human use through a vast man-made infrastructure of reservoirs, aqueducts, dams, pipelines, purification and treatment plants, and other devices. Unfortunately, the US water system is currently in bad condition—underfunded, aging, limited in its capacity, and not adaptable to our changing climate. The crumbling system means leaky pipes, polluted water, and poor conservation, all of which costs the nation billions of dollars annually. Particularly in arid regions, the infrastructure is not designed to capture rainwater for municipal use but rather, as in such cities as Los Angeles, to remove it as quickly as possible and send it to the ocean. The ironic result is that Los Angeles imports most of its water rather than capturing and using the significant amount of storm water it receives.[8]

Major new investments in infrastructure are needed to render our national water system adequate for the demands of the twenty-first century. Fortunately, some innovative infrastructure development is occurring in cities across the country, including Philadelphia (which is in the midst of a twenty-year project to build massive green infrastructure to capture water), Milwaukee (a world water hub for infrastructure and conservation), Los Angeles (pioneering a multiagency approach to conservation), and New York (focusing on green infrastructure development).

Meanwhile, growing regions of the world—including parts of the United States—can expect to experience steadily worsening levels

---

7 E-mail, Cindy Hoffman, Defenders of Wildlife, May 13, 2011.

8 "In a region that imports water, much goes to waste," *Los Angeles Times*, http://articles.latimes.com/2010/dec/24/local/la-me-water-storms-20101224, accessed on May 15, 2011.

of water shortage, with wide-ranging consequences. For example, Las Vegas County, with a population of 2 million, will lose the power generated by Hoover Dam when Lake Mead's water elevation falls below 1,050 feet (the height of the lake's "upper intake" system, which feeds the dam). With Lake Mead at 1,086 feet during the filming of *Last Call at the Oasis* in 2011—and falling by around ten feet every year—that is only four years away.

QUALITY: WILL THE WATER OF LIFE MAKE US SICK?

Water shortages are not the only challenge facing our water supply. There are also serious quality problems that belie the widespread assumption that residents of advanced countries, such as the United States, no longer need to worry about the purity and safety of their drinking water.

Two historic laws regulate the safety of water supplies in the United States: the Safe Drinking Water Act (SDWA) and the Clean Water Act (CWA). Passed by Congress in 1974, the SDWA regulates ground and surface waters used for human consumption. Administered by the Environmental Protection Agency (EPA), the law allows the agency to establish, amend, and update standards for public water systems (subject to review and change by congressional and Supreme Court decisions). However, 40 million citizens use well water, not municipal water, which isn't regulated by the SDWA.

The Clean Water Act, originally passed by Congress in 1972, regulates pollutants and protects surface waters (rivers, lakes, and so on). Permits must be obtained from the EPA to discharge pollutants into these waters. The CWA represents an important milestone in the nation's commitment to protecting our water supply. However, the existence of a law is not enough to produce results on the ground. According to a 2009 report in the *New York Times,* the CWA was violated half a million times in the previous five years.[9]

A wide variety of pollutants can be found in the water that Americans rely on for personal consumption. For example, hexavalent chromium (chromium-6), the "Erin Brockovich contaminant" featured in the eponymous film, is a carcinogen used in paints, dyes, and plastics, as an anticorrosive agent, and in welding. It traditionally has entered drinking water from leaks at industrial plants and hazardous waste sites.[10] Now it is being introduced into both municipal and well water systems through "fracking," as discussed below.[11] A study by the Environmental Working Group found hexavalent chromium in thirty-one of thirty-five municipal drinking water systems, with Honolulu, Hawaii; Riverside, California; Norman, Oklahoma; Madison, Wisconsin; and San Jose, California, topping the list.[12]

The gas-extraction process of hydraulic fracturing, also known as fracking, is spreading across the United States. Chemicals mixed with water are drilled into shale rock to release deeply trapped natural gas. Due to the so-called Halliburton loophole in the SDWA, which was created by the 2005 energy bill, companies are not required to publicly disclose the chemicals used in this process. But water in and near fracking sites has been contaminated with high

---

9 Charles Duhigg, "Clean Water Laws Are Neglected, at a Cost in Suffering," *New York Times,* September 12, 2009, www.nytimes.com/2009/09/13/us/13water.html, accessed May 11, 2011.

10 "Draft Public Health Goal for Hexavalent Chromium," Office of Environmental Health Hazard Assessment, California Environmental Protection Agency, August 2009, http://oehha.ca.gov/water/phg/pdf/HexChromfacts082009.pdf, accessed May 11, 2011.

11 Joyce Nelson, "Ugly Reality of Fracking," *Greenmuze* blog, www.greenmuze.com/climate/energy/2562-ugly-reality-of-fracking.html, accessed January 7, 2012.

12 Wendy Koch, "Study: Tap Water in US Cities Has Probable Carcinogen," *USA Today,* December 20, 2010, http://content.usatoday.com/communities/greenhouse/post/2010/12/tap-water-of-many-us-cities-has-probable-carcinogen-study/1?POE=click-refer, accessed May 12, 2011.

levels of ethane, benzene, methane, and hexavalent chromium. Communities affected by fracking have been plagued by severely polluted groundwater (including flammable drinking water due to methane in the water)[13] and a host of health problems for residents, including cancer and brain tumors.

The House Energy and Commerce Committee's 2011 investigation of fracking "found that 14 of the nation's most active hydraulic fracturing companies used 866 million gallons of hydraulic fracturing products—not including water. More than 650 of these products contained chemicals that are known or possible human carcinogens, regulated under the Safe Drinking Water Act, or are listed as hazardous air pollutants."[14]

Atrazine is another widespread contaminant of American drinking water. The second–most common herbicide used on corn— which is itself the number-one crop in the United States—atrazine is found in 94 percent of all drinking water tested by the USDA.[15] A known endocrine disruptor that causes birth defects and cancer, atrazine is banned in the European Union and is currently under review at the EPA.[16]

Concentrated animal feeding operations (CAFOs) are a significant source of water pollution. These massive factory farms generate 500 million tons of manure annually, equivalent to many American cities. However, they are not required to treat the waste in the same

---

13 Abrahm Lustgarten, "Scientific Study Links Flammable Drinking Water to Fracking," ProPublica, May 9, 2011, www.propublica.org/article/scientific-study-links-flammable -drinking-water-to-fracking, accessed May 12, 2011.

14 Ian Urbina, "Chemicals Were Injected into Wells," *New York Times,* April 16, 2011, www.nytimes.com/2011/04/17/science/earth/17gas.html?_r=3&emc=eta1, accessed May 12, 2011.

15 "What's on My Food?" Pesticide Action Network, www.whatsonmyfood.org/food .jsp?food=WU, accessed May 11, 2011.

16 "Pesticides and Birth Defects," Pesticide Action Network, www.panna.org/resources/ panups/panup_20090409#1, accessed May 13, 2011.

way as municipalities. Instead the waste is stored in lagoons and later spread on nearby farmland, where it seeps into and contaminates local water sources and kills aquatic life.[17] Other agricultural processes also contribute to water pollution. For example, nitrates found in animal waste and fertilizer (and associated with so-called blue baby syndrome) have contaminated rural and urban California drinking water, including in Los Angeles.[18]

Yet another form of pollution is pharmaceutical chemicals that find their way into water supplies after being discarded at home, dumped or excreted into sewage systems, or carelessly disposed of by manufacturers. Wastewater treatment plants are unable to properly treat these contaminants in the drinking water. According to an AP investigation, the drinking water used by 41 million Americans contains measurable amounts of pharmaceuticals, including antibiotics, mood stabilizers, sex hormones, and anticonvulsants.[19]

Storm water runoff, a growing problem because of increased flooding due to climate change, is the number-one source for contaminants of municipal drinking water. City systems cannot capture and treat all of the flood water, which means more polluted water is dumped into oceans, rivers, and other regional water sources.

THE ENERGY-WATER NEXUS

Americans have long been accustomed to the notion of an energy shortage caused by growing demand, dwindling supplies of fossil

17 "Water Sentinels: Factory Farms," Sierra Club, www.sierraclub.org/watersentinels/factoryfarms.aspx, accessed May 12, 2011.

18 Julia Scott, "Nitrate Contamination Spreading in California Communities," California Watch, May 13, 2010, http://californiawatch.org/nitrate-contamination-spreading-california-communities, accessed May 12, 2011.

19 Jeff Donn, Martha Mendoza, and Justin Pritchard, "Pharmaceuticals Lurking in US Drinking Water," MSNBC, March 10, 2008, www.msnbc.msn.com/id/23503485/ns/health-health_care/t/pharmaceuticals-lurking-us-drinking-water, accessed May 11, 2011.

fuels, and our troubling dependence on unstable, sometimes hostile foreign regimes for oil, gas, and other resources. Less familiar, however, is the profound interconnection between energy use and water use, which experts have begun calling "the energy-water nexus." This nexus is emerging as a critical issue for public policy, business leaders, and economic thinkers.

The connections between energy and water run in several directions. In many regions, especially arid ones, energy is used to move water to where it needs to be. As we've already noted in the case of Los Angeles, this is often due to our failure to invest in systems that use available groundwater and the capturing of storm water rather than "importing" water over long distances via pipelines. The California State Water Project pumps water 2,000 feet over mountains, using a lot of energy and vast amounts of money in the process. And 90 percent of all the energy used in California's agricultural sector is for pumping groundwater for irrigation—another huge, largely wasted expense.[20]

Furthermore, moving water around is difficult as well as costly. Water is very heavy compared to its economic value, which means that transporting water long distances generally is not economically feasible. For example, a barrel of oil weighs about 125 kilograms (275 pounds) and has been valued at between $35 and $145 on the world market in the past ten years.[21] The same volume of water weighs about 159 kilograms (350 pounds), and in one (rather expensive) US municipality is sold to households for about 14 cents. It's easy to see that the lower value of water makes moving it highly impractical from an economic standpoint.

---

20 R. Cohen, B. Nelson, and G. Wolff, "Energy Down the Drain: The Hidden Costs of California's Water Supply," National Resources Defense Council, Oakland, California, 2004, www.nrdc.org/water/conservation/edrain/execsum.asp, accessed May 15, 2011.

21 World Economic Forum, Water-Energy.

Furthermore, unlike with some other commodities, a global market for water does not exist. This means that water resources must be optimized and managed locally. This makes water very different from greenhouse gas emissions. A reduction in greenhouse gas emissions in Brazil theoretically could offset increasing emissions in the United States, but the abundance of freshwater in the Brazilian Amazon is not helpful for the drought-prone American Southwest.

On the other side of the energy-water nexus is the use of water to produce energy, for example, through hydroelectric dams. In the United States, about half the water withdrawn is for cooling power plants. US power plants withdrew enough freshwater each day in 2008 to supply 60 to 170 cities the size of New York.[22] Beyond cooling power plants, water is used to produce natural gas and liquid fuels from raw materials. On average, producing one liter of oil requires one to three liters of water. Producing gasoline from oil sands requires from three to fifty-five liters of water per liter of gasoline.

At the same time, water scarcity is already a limiting factor for energy production. In 2011 the Texas drought caused at least one power plant to go offline. In 2007 the drought in the Southeast United States forced much lower production in energy. Water shortages in France and the United States also have threatened nuclear power production.

Water used for energy production can total 250 gallons per citizen daily.[23] Power plants use a significant amount of water for cool-

22 K. Averyt, J. Fisher, A. Huber-Lee, A. Lewis, J. Macknick, N. Madden, J. Rogers, and S. Tellinghuisen, "Freshwater Use by US Power Plants: Electricity's Thirst for a Precious Resource," Energy and Water in a Warming World Initiative, Union of Concerned Scientists, Cambridge, MA, November 2011, www.ucsusa.org/assets/documents/clean_energy/ew3/ew3-freshwater-use-by-us-power-plants.pdf, accessed January 7, 2012.

23 "The Worldwide 'Thirst' for Clean Drinking Water," NPR, April 11, 2011, www.npr.org/2011/04/11/135241362/the-worldwide-thirst-for-clean-drinking-water, accessed May 11, 2011.

ing, with serious environmental consequences. Millions of fish are killed, and the used water is dumped back into its original source at a warmer temperature, affecting the ecosystem.

The impact of the energy-water nexus means that the manufacture of virtually any consumer product consumes a startling quantity of water. Examples of this "hidden water" in common products include the 1,800 gallons of water consumed in producing one pound of beef; the 1,000 gallons used in producing a gallon of wine; and the 700 gallons of water used in manufacturing a single cotton T-shirt.

The various forms of resource consumption practiced in advanced technological societies are so closely intertwined that it seems safe to conclude that there is no way to truly solve our energy problems without also solving our water problems—and vice versa.

WATER AND AGRICULTURE

Agriculture is a major user of ground- and surface water in the United States, accounting for 80 percent of the nation's consumptive water use and over 90 percent in many western states.

California offers a vivid illustration of the dependence of modern agriculture on massive water consumption. The state is America's greatest producer of agricultural goods despite being largely arid, relying on huge, expensive in-state irrigation systems. California's Central Valley alone grows one-quarter of all the food produced in the United States, with an annual value of over $28 billion.[24] This naturally arid region is fed water through a maze of irrigation pipes, dams, and other water diversion mechanisms scattered around the

---

24 E-mail, Jay Famiglietti, May 11, 2011.

state, all directed toward watering these fields. Fifty percent of this water comes from the San Joaquin–Sacramento Delta, which also provides water for 23 million Californians.[25] In addition, about 20 percent of the nation's groundwater demand is supplied from pumping Central Valley aquifers, making it the second–most pumped aquifer system in the United States. Much of this water is provided to farmers at cheap rates because of government subsidies. An Environmental Working Group report found that nearly 7,000 Central Valley farms received water subsidies of about $416 million.[26]

The San Francisco Bay delta is the heart of the state's irrigation system, providing water to 22 million Californians and over 7 million acres of farmland.[27] It is created where the Sierra Mountains snowpack feeds into the San Joaquin and Sacramento Rivers. These rivers flow into the bay delta, but the San Joaquin's flow is generally inhibited by a dam built upstream for agricultural purposes. It is very difficult to predict exactly how climate change will affect this water system in the future.

The delta is also home to two endangered species—the king salmon and the delta smelt—that have come to symbolize the environmental problems of the bay delta system. The fish are killed by pumps and dry rivers, along with contaminants and invasive species.

California's multibillion-dollar agricultural industry is critical to the nation. However, better techniques must be employed to save water and protect water sources. The practice of growing water-

---

25 Sue McClurg, "A Briefing on the Bay-Delta and CALFED," Water Education Foundation, www.watereducation.org/userfiles/ABriefingontheDeltaandCALFED2.pdf, accessed May 11, 2011.

26 "California Water Subsidies," Environmental Work Group, http://archive.ewg.org/reports/Watersubsidies/execsumm.php, accessed May 11, 2011.

27 "A Healthy and Sustainable Vision for California," Sierra Club, www.sierraclub.org/ca/water/index.asp, accessed May 16, 2011.

intensive crops in the arid Central Valley makes little sense and is ultimately unsustainable. Water conservation, better agricultural practices, more realistic water pricing, and a shift to more appropriate crops will all help to conserve and protect the state's dwindling water sources.

California isn't the only region of the United States where agriculture is stressing water supplies. For example, the vast Ogallala Aquifer in the Midwest is under increasing pressure from the massive corn industry, which is draining and polluting the aquifer.

THE IMPACT OF CLIMATE CHANGE

It's difficult to estimate exactly how greatly climate change will affect worldwide water supplies in the next century. However, most climate scientists believe there will be more severe droughts and less snowpack in already arid regions like the western United States as well as intensified storms and flooding in wet areas, such as the eastern United States. For example, Jay Famiglietti suggests that by 2100, 90 percent of the California Sierra Mountains snowpack—which produces 25 percent of Southern California's water—will be gone.[28] According to the National Resources Defense Council, 1,100 counties across the United States—one-third of all counties in the lower forty-eight states—can expect to face water shortages by the year 2050 because of climate change, with four hundred counties experiencing severe shortages. The climate change–induced intensified water cycle will mean that groundwater, the oldest and most vulnerable water source, will not be renewed by rainfall to the same extent as in the past.

---

28 "Climate Choices," Union of Concerned Scientists—USA, www.climatechoices.org/impacts_water, accessed May 12, 2011; phone conversation with Jay Famiglietti, May 10, 2011.

Energy Secretary Steven Chu offered a dire warning for California about depleted water sources due to climate change. According to a *Los Angeles Times* article, Chu observed, "I don't think the American public has gripped in its gut what could happen. We're looking at a scenario where there's no more agriculture in California. I don't actually see how they can keep their cities going."[29]

According to the Intergovernmental Panel on Climate Change, the global situation is equally dire. "By 2050, more than a billion people in Asia could face water shortages. By 2080, water shortages could threaten 1.1 billion to 3.2 billion people, depending on the level of greenhouse gases that cars and industry spew into the air."[30]

POTENTIAL SOLUTIONS: DESALINATION, RECYCLING

Considering the virtually limitless supply of ocean water, desalination is sometimes touted as an easy solution to the problem of drinking-water shortages. According to an International Desalination Association Report, there are over 13,000 desalination plants worldwide. The largest US plant is in Tampa, Florida. However, the desalination process is expensive and polluting, producing both greenhouse gas emissions and waste brine that is almost as difficult to dispose of as spent nuclear fuel. As Peter Gleick of the Pacific Institute has observed, water conservation is much cheaper and more effective than trying to quench our desire for more water by "manufacturing" it.

Recycling of water that has been used in residential or commercial sewage systems is technically feasible but often controversial

---

29 Jim Tankersley, "California Farms, Vineyards in Peril from Warming, US Energy Secretary Warns," *Los Angeles Times,* February 4, 2009, http://articles.latimes.com/2009/feb/04/local/me-warming4, accessed May 11, 2011.

30 Associated Press, "Top Scientists Warn of Water Shortages and Disease Linked to Global Warming," *New York Times,* March 12, 2007, www.nytimes.com/2007/03/12/science/earth/12climate.html, accessed May 11, 2011.

because of its distasteful connotations. Despite the psychological challenges, water recycling is already occurring nationwide. According to WateReuse, a desalination and water reuse organization, so-called toilet-to-tap recycling is being practiced in Mesa and Tucson, Arizona; the Orange County and West Basin water districts in California; West Palm Beach, Florida; El Paso, Texas; and a number of other locations in the United States.

Outside the United States, the city-state of Singapore is practicing water recycling on a major scale. Singapore's NEWater program uses reverse osmosis and ultraviolet technologies to produce around 30 percent of the city's water from used water sources.

BOTTLED WATER—PART OF THE SOLUTION OR PART OF THE PROBLEM?

The United States is the world's largest consumer of bottled water. As Peter Gleick wrote in 2010, "In the past 25 years, American consumption of tap water has dropped by more than 35 gallons per person per year, replaced largely by bottled water and carbonated soft drinks. We now drink more bottled water than milk or juice—nearly 9 billion gallons last year, at a high cost to consumers and the environment."[31] Worldwide, 200 billion liters of bottled water were consumed in 2008.[32] The largest bottled water companies globally are Nestle, Coca-Cola, PepsiCo, Danone, and Crystal Geyser.[33]

31 Peter H. Gleick, "US Water System Needs Better Enforcement, Smart Investment to Ensure Quality," *Washington Post,* June 15, 2010, www.washingtonpost.com/wp-dyn/content/article/2010/06/14/AR2010061404637.html, accessed May 12, 2011.

32 Alice McKeown, "Bottled Water Consumption Growth Slows," Vital Signs, February 25, 2010, http://vitalsigns.worldwatch.org/vs-trend/bottled-water-consumption-growth -slows, accessed May 12, 2011.

33 "Top Selling Soft Drink Companies," AdBrands.net, www.adbrands.net/sectors/sector _softdrinks.htm, accessed May 16, 2011.

People are turning to bottled water in large part because their trust in municipal water systems is declining. However, bottled water is not regulated as tap water is. In the United States, it is a consumer product overseen by the Food and Drug Administration, and the regulations governing it are generally weaker than those governing municipal water systems. And from a consumer standpoint, bottled water is scarcely worth its relatively exorbitant cost. Up to 45 percent of the bottled water sold is simply tap water packaged in a plastic bottle that leaches contaminants. What's worse, Peter Gleick tracked more than one hundred cases of bottled water recalls involving such contaminants as coliform bacteria, sanitizers, mold, glass particles, and cricket parts.

It's clear that bottled water doesn't offer a solution to either the quantity or quality problems with our water supply. Just the opposite: the market for bottled water may actually hurt efforts to defend, protect, and improve public water systems. In 2008 Americans spent an estimated $11.2 billion on bottled water—which ironically is almost exactly the same amount that experts say is needed to improve annual maintenance of our water infrastructure. Transferring that flow of money from its current use to a well-crafted infrastructure maintenance program would be a far better investment in our water future.

WARS OVER WATER?

Talk of the energy-water nexus and of worsening water shortages in many parts of the world leads people inevitably to wonder: Will the wars of the twenty-first century be fought over water, the way some of the wars of past centuries were fought over resources ranging from gold to oil? Some experts in geopolitics have confidently predicted the coming advent of an era of "water wars."

If wars over water are imminent, one might assume that the already volatile Middle East might be a likely kindling zone. And it's true that water supplies in that arid part of the world are under significant pressure. The Jordan River, which runs along the border between Jordan, Israel, and the West Bank, is down to just 2 percent of its historical flow due to overuse by everyone in the region and a growing infrastructure of dams, reservoirs, and pipelines impeding and draining its waters. The Yarmouk River to the east is also struggling. Both of these rivers feed into the Dead Sea, whose levels continue to drop because of the rivers' depleted flows, tourism, and mineral extraction by Israelis and Jordanians. There are plans for expanded development around the sea as well, which will put further pressures on it.[34]

Yet, as Aaron Wolf, professor of geology in the Department of Geosciences at Oregon State University, explains in the film *Last Call at the Oasis,* not only has there been no Arab-Israeli war over water, but there is actually significant cooperative work under way to conserve regional water supplies and use them fairly and responsibly. In fact, Wolf's research into global water controversies reveals that for every conflict over water, there are dozens of instances of nations, states, and tribes that have negotiated peaceful settlements involving the sharing of water resources. It's as if people recognize not just the economic value of water but also its sanctity as the source and guarantor of human life, and therefore are loath to take up arms to seize it.

Does this mean there will be no water wars in the decades to come? That would be too sanguine a conclusion. History presents

---

34 "Dead Sea," Friends of the Earth Middle East, http://foeme.org/www/?module=projects &record_id=21, accessed May 12, 2011.

such a steady stream of human folly that it's easy to imagine some future controversy over water rights erupting into needless and unproductive violence—if not in the Middle East, then perhaps on the border between China and Russia, India and Pakistan, or even the United States and Mexico. The possibility makes it even more urgent that we do all we can to mitigate the onrushing water crises we face as a species—and begin doing it today.

2

EXPLORING
OASIS

The Making of
Last Call at the Oasis

Jessica Yu

Jessica Yu is a director of both documentaries and scripted films. She won an Oscar for Best Documentary Short for *Breathing Lessons*, a film about Mark O'Brien, the poet who was confined to an iron lung. Her other films include the cult comedy *Ping Pong Playa* and the documentary features *Protagonist, In the Realms of the Unreal*, and HBO's *The Living Museum*. She also has directed various television shows, including *The West Wing, Grey's Anatomy,* and *Parenthood*.

Currently (January 2012) Yu is finishing a film about the Gorongosa National Park Restoration Project in Mozambique.

I'm not one of those directors who knew they wanted to direct from the time they could hold a camera. But I loved movies, partly because I like storytelling, partly because I always liked making things—anything at all, right down to the chicken coops my family built when I was a kid. Sometimes it still surprises me that I do what I do, but in retrospect becoming a filmmaker was a sensible, if unpremeditated, decision.

I grew up in Northern California. My dad's an oncologist, and my mother is a historian who has written books under the name Connie Young Yu about the history of the Chinese in California. So I grew up with a sense of history and how it shapes our lives and perceptions.

My parents were both politically active in the antiwar movement, especially my mom. I don't remember any other Asian-American families being involved the way ours was. When I was a kid, my brother and I were taken on picket lines, we boycotted grapes in support of Cesar Chavez and the farmworkers' movement, and we would tag along with our mom when she went to the Peace Center in Palo Alto to help with draft counseling, planning demonstrations, and so on. Of course, I didn't always understand it all. I remember thinking that my mom was working on *giraffe* counseling. And when my parents got involved in politically focused "guerrilla theater," of course I thought it was *gorilla* theater. My parents felt it was important to stand up for one's principles, but they didn't preach to us about it. Mostly we kids sat on the sidelines, reading *Mad* magazine and chiming in on the chants we recognized.

After studying English at Yale, I really didn't know what I wanted to do. So I started working in film production, not really seeing it as a lifelong career decision but as sporadic, interesting work that I could fit into my fencing schedule. Strange but true: for a short while, my life was ruled by the international fencing circuit. I come from a family of competitive fencers (my mom still coaches). After college, I was still competing, and it was hard to have a nine-to-five job when I had to fly off to Frankfurt or Bulgaria—usually to get schooled in matches by some hardcore Eastern Europeans.

I started out as a production assistant. Not having gone to film school, I was learning on the job. My first job was a frozen food commercial. For six hours, I arranged noodles on plastic forks. I also reparked producers' cars and went on prop runs. It was not exactly glamorous, but it offered a humbling introduction to the whole notion of what it takes to make even the shortest piece of film.

As I continued to work, film grew more appealing. The first shoot where I actually got to handle a piece of equipment that wasn't a frozen noodle was a documentary shoot where I assisted with everything from research to sound recording. The film was Freida Lee Mock's film *Maya Lin: A Strong, Clear Vision,* which went on to win the Academy Award in 1995. I liked the intimacy of documentary production. Unlike commercials with their large crews, documentaries are often an all-hands-on-deck process. When the crew is small, the learning curve is much steeper—and everyone parks their own car.

Over time, I discovered that filmmaking was like a grown-up version of something I'd enjoyed as a child—show-and-tell in school. You bring something to class that you think is cool, and then you get to show it and explain why you think it's cool. Filmmaking is about the same impulse: to capture what fascinates, delights, excites, or shocks you about a subject and communicate it to an audience.

It helps me to remember that simple goal, especially when I'm in danger of getting sidetracked by all the minutia of production. As I work on the movie—developing it, scripting it, filming it, editing it—I'm keeping track of all those "aha" moments, moments of humor, moments of beauty, moments of recognition, moments of revelation. At the same time, I'm drawing connections among those moments, and trying to arrange them in a way that can enhance their cumulative impact. I'm always thinking, "I wish I had known A before I knew B," or "Wouldn't it be great to see X, Y, and Z next to each other?" And in editing and putting together the film, I get to rearrange those moments to make the ideal journey for my audience—to capture and convey the way I would have liked to have experienced the story.

To me, this concept of orchestrating the perfect journey for the viewer is a good guiding principle for a filmmaker, because it keeps me mindful of the people who are physically sitting there in that dark theater, watching this movie play out on the screen. As a director, you're asking those people to make a commitment to you and to your film. As those kind strangers look on, how should the story play out? What should they know at this point in the movie? What shouldn't they know? How will they feel when they put these things together? And how can we not just inform them but also engage and entertain them?

Of course, engaging the viewer was a crucial challenge in making an issues film like *Last Call at the Oasis*. From the beginning, we knew that we had to tell stories. If we just filled the screen with graphs and numbers and lectures, we couldn't really expect people to become emotionally involved. Audiences connect with characters, not facts.

I got involved in *Last Call* through Diane Weyermann, executive vice president at Participant Media. I had known Diane through her years at Sundance when she was head of the documentary program there, and worked with her on the Sundance Documentary Fund. I always admired Diane's taste, and she's well-known for having unshakable integrity, especially when it comes to supporting films and filmmakers. At Participant, Diane is focused on making nonfiction films about the most crucial challenges facing the planet and society today.

One day over lunch, Diane mentioned that water was a topic that was on Participant's radar, and she wondered if I would be interested in pursuing a film on this subject with them. I had two immediate reactions. From the film-geek perspective, I thought it would be amazing to make a film about water because of its visual interest. My mind filled with visions of waterfalls and perfect lakes and fountains shooting cascades of glittering drops. (In making the film, we came to call this "water porn.")

And my other reaction was that if water was one of Participant Media's top priorities, then whatever was happening out there with the water crisis must be a lot worse than I might expect. So right away I experienced a disconnect: our idealized vision of water is pristine and infinite, but our real-world, collective impact on the water supply has left it in quite a different state. This immediately interested me—the contradiction between how we view and how we treat this most essential of resources.

In some stories, the perfect journey ends in an emotional catharsis. And in other stories, grasping a big concept is most important. I would argue that a movie like *Last Call* has to combine more than one sort of impact. As it presents a mosaic of scenes, stories, personalities, and images, I hope it generates an accumulation of understanding that leads to a final, most important "aha" moment—the moment when viewers can actually see all facets of the water issue together.

At the Toronto Film Festival, program director Thom Powers called *Last Call at the Oasis* a "feel-angry movie," which he later amended to "feel-smart movie." I was rather partial to both labels, since they emphasize the "feel" part. We wanted to make *Last Call* an emotional film as well as an educational one. My hope was for people to connect viscerally and personally to the water crisis. We wanted to bring water problems into the open, to show the impact on the lives of real people—to bring oft-hidden abstractions into the light of day where we can finally see what's going on.

The issues related to water are so interconnected and complex that if you don't have a certain basic understanding of those connections, the final picture can leave things more muddied than when you started. We didn't want people to walk away from the film feeling more confused than before; we wanted people to come out feeling smarter at the end of the movie, having followed all the various threads and clues in assembling the big picture of the water crisis and its impact on our future. In the end, we hope that knowledge will satisfy and empower audiences, so people don't just want to throw in the towel. (A lot of towels were tossed in the process of researching this film—and later retrieved.) If we can understand something as complex and crucial as the water crisis, then we are capable of making things better.

First, our production team—me, producer Elise Pearlstein, and associate producer Sandra Keats—needed to educate ourselves. We were privileged to be able to go to the source: the scientists and educators who have been working on this front for a long time. They're the unsung heroes of *Last Call at the Oasis*. They've been in the trenches, studying the decline of our global water supply and the pressures it faces, from waste to pollution. And they've also played a crucial role in educating citizens, policy makers, and business leaders about the growing risks to the water supplies on which life depends.

To me, these scientists are heroic not just because of what they've discovered but because they're extending themselves beyond the traditional scientist's role. Their job description does not include holding press conferences and trying to sound the clarion call. Yet many of the scientists we've encountered have come to adopt a moral imperative in relation to what they've learned. The sentiment they expressed was, "If we don't get this out to the public, we're responsible for what might continue to happen."

It's quite a contrast to the traditional academic approach of drawing the line at the door of the lab. Several of the scientists we talked to mentioned that they face criticism from colleagues who disapprove of their decision to reach out to the public, to connect the dots, and to suggest to their students that public advocacy is now part of the scientist's job. But if a scientist makes no attempt to publicize his work, chances are it's a tree falling in the forest without a sound.

Jay Famiglietti, one of the scientists in the film, shared with us a shocking statistic—not about water shortages, but about scientific research. Jay said the average number of citations for a published research paper—which is often the result of years of painstaking work—is one. For Jay, this speaks to the futility of relying on peer-reviewed scientific publications in getting out crucial messages. As Jay told us, if scientists don't even read one another's work, how on earth can they expect it to have an impact on the public? So reaching out through the popular media—including films like *Last Call*—is an increasingly important extension of the scientist's role. Although as Jay freely admits, most scientists aren't very good at it yet: "We didn't go to school to become great communicators."

With *Last Call*, we knew we had an opportunity to provide a bridge for these scientists and help make the research accessible to the general public. The first step, of course, was learning about the role of water in our world and the ways in which our supply is imperiled. It's a complex subject and a moving target. Some of the indicators of change are obvious and measurable: the depth of Lake Mead, glacial retreat in the Himalayas, the amount of rainfall in the Sahel. Others, like traces of new contaminants in the water supply, are much more subtle. We absorbed all we could from our experts and the existing research to distill and determine what was most important in the latest trends and changes.

At the same time, I was searching for stories that were relevant and compelling—stories filled with dynamic visuals and strong characters that would also capture important truths about our relationship to this essential resource.

Some of the examples of water abuse and conflict we ended up using felt almost inevitable—Las Vegas, for example. Vegas offers an irresistibly graphic example of irrational water use—the prototypical, artificial "desert oasis"—although its story holds surprises as well.

We were also looking for "the unusual suspects," which meant that Elise, Sandra, and I spent months talking to people and scouring books, publications, and the Internet. It's rare to discover a story that's both compelling and relevant, and also linked to a person who's interesting and engaging on film. Sometimes you hear people coming out of a great documentary saying things like, "Truth is better than fiction," or "You can't make this stuff up." Sometimes that means the filmmakers stumbled upon a gold mine of a story right off the bat, but more often it means they put in a lot of effort to find that perfect truth, turning over countless stones and following numerous leads. (For example, Elise spent weeks "politely stalking" the mind-bogglingly busy water and legal activist Erin Brockovich, but that's a story of its own.)

In this case, I'd say we spent six months researching the water crisis and developing our film treatment—a kind of blueprint for the sequence of stories we planned to tell. This was followed by a solid eight months of production, during which research was still taking place, and then months of editing, follow-up filming, graphics, and other work to get the picture into final form.

From the beginning, I was fascinated by the whole psychology behind the water crisis. Problems such as drought, pollution, contamination, competition for resources, and privatization aren't new; they've existed since before civilization. Still, we've failed to address them in any consistent, systematic way. In the movie, we wanted to explore this paradoxical behavior: Why don't we act in ways that are in our own self-interest, especially when it comes to something as crucial as water?

Compounding the damage caused by our collective inertia is the other aspect of the water crisis I found most jarring: the shockingly short time frame in which we will face devastating consequences. Growing up in California, I was aware of drought and the need to conserve, but permanent, environmentally crippling, end-of-business-as-usual changes in the water supply seemed a far-off notion. But scientist Jay Famiglietti estimates that the aquifer in the Central Valley, where a quarter of our nation's food is produced, might be depleted in as little as sixty years. And we learned that of the more than 80,000 chemicals used in the United States, many of which end up in our water supplies every day, only five are regulated under the Toxic Substances Control Act. Faced with these realities, we soon grew to share the sense of urgency with our scientists and other experts.

I was lucky to have the help of a fantastic creative team, including Elise, Sandra, and Kim Roberts, our editor. They were my partners in solving the various technical and narrative challenges we faced. In the end, we organized the movie around major aspects of the water crisis, starting with the most familiar—drought—and gradually trying to open viewers' eyes to the surprising realities beneath a seemingly well-understood problem. This principle of continually surprising the audience without confusing or alienating them is an important one that we used to help shape the entire structure of the picture.

We start with Vegas, which illustrates the drought problem— but of course now it's drought compounded by climate change and overuse and population growth. So it's water scarcity squared. Then we move from Vegas to a series of revelations about California and the conflict among agriculture, the environment, and growth in the world's fifth-largest economy. From there we move on to Australia, which has an agricultural economy that's starting to collapse under the weight of its untenable water problems. As Peter Gleick of the Pacific Institute says, "The Australia of today is the California of tomorrow." So our section on drought begins with the familiar and then escalates into a nightmarish potential future. Underlying these stories is the question: How could something this monumental be happening with so little public awareness?

Next we have the section about water quality, pollution, and contamination issues. Here, again, we start with examples that may be familiar to people, but then move on to reveal that the problem is more serious and widespread than most of us realize. For example, many of the contaminated-water problems affecting people originate in well water, which may seem like a fairly isolated rural concern. But the reality is that over 40 million people in the United States depend on well water, which is rarely or never tested for purity and safety.

After depicting the problems plaguing public sources of water, we turn to the subject of bottled water, which is perhaps the trickiest turn in the film. It might seem obvious that bottled water is the rational alternative to risky water from the tap, but it's not—in fact, the bottled water marketers have played on our fear of what's in our water to sell us something that is often identical to tap water, less frequently tested, and environmentally costly. And that leads naturally to the last section of the film, which is about the psychology of water use and its impact on our search for *real* solutions to the water crisis.

In trying to create the "perfect journey," in which the film parallels our own route of discovery, we encountered quite a series of "aha" moments. Our first international shoot was in Singapore, which we had targeted as one of the few places in the world where water is being managed in an extremely thoughtful, comprehensive, and sustainable way. (We also went there so that we could attend the World Toilet Summit—yes, there is such a thing!)

What we saw in Singapore taught us how actions, and action on both the personal scale and the larger policy scale, are required to address a problem of this scope. Government agencies are investing in water-conserving and water-purifying technology, capturing rainfall, recycling water, and reducing waste in myriad ways. The water technology Singapore has fostered has spawned a billion-dollar industry.

Singapore also prices water realistically to reflect its actual value and cost. This has had an impact on the behavior of individual citizens, who monitor their use and rely on water-saving devices to cut down on needless water flow. When we spoke to people on the streets of Singapore, they were amazingly well informed about water issues. Ask the average American how much her monthly water bill is, and chances are she can't tell you. But the average Singaporean is as familiar with her water bill as her phone or cable bill.

All in all, Singapore is doing a remarkable job of tackling the water crisis head-on. I found it both inspiring and daunting. Inspiring, because it shows that there are real solutions to the problems we face. But at the same time, the example of Singapore is singular. The nation-state is tiny, it's far more autocratic than other larger, developed nations, and the push to manage its water situation was propelled by tremendous political will. Singapore wanted to escape its reliance on neighboring Malaysia for its water supply, a goal behind which the government and the people could unite.

By contrast, the United States is large, messy, and governed by an unwieldy assortment of water laws that vary from state to state. We can't even agree that we indeed face water issues. So acknowledging that there is a problem is the first step. Perhaps our country needs a water self-help program (WA—Water Anonymous?).

One Singaporean effort that we could learn from here is its educational program on water. Every Singaporean schoolkid visits the NEWater recycled water plant or the educational center Marina Barrage to learn about the importance of water. The Public Utility Board motto is "Conserve, protect, enjoy," which makes the message easy to understand. When kids grow up with an awareness of how precious water is and the need for everyone to treat it with respect, their behavior changes. I've seen it in my own children (they're seven and ten years old) as a result of my involvement with *Last Call*. When they're brushing their teeth, they rinse their teeth using a shared glass of water; they carry reusable water bottles to the skateboard park; they don't flush every time they pee in the toilet. These are little actions, but taken over the course of a lifetime, they can add up significantly.

We experienced other hopeful revelations in the process of making the film. For example, we heard a lot of hyperbole about how the next wars will be triggered by competition for water. But Aaron Wolf, the professor at Oregon State University who has been mapping water conflicts around the world, told us that while water problems exacerbate tensions, very few wars are actually waged over water. ("You can only live for three days without water. . . . It's pretty hard to mount an invasion around that.") What Wolf has found is that water's importance can actually transcend political conflicts—competing parties will find ways to compromise over its distribution and use. Our filming with Friends of the Earth Middle East introduced us to this kind of unlikely compromise between Palestinians, Israelis, and Jordanians. Who would have thought that the Middle East would provide a hopeful example of peaceful conflict resolution?

I don't think we're necessarily headed toward a water Armageddon. But the problems humankind faces around water are tremendously complex, and they demand far more attention than they've been getting.

Can these problems be solved? I think scientists Jay Famiglietti and Tyrone Hayes answer that question best at the very end of the movie, when they say that the water crisis may not be a *solvable* problem, but it's a *manageable* problem. In that respect, it resembles the related problem of climate change, which is probably no longer reversible but can be managed so as to mitigate the damage. If we think about the water crisis in terms of slowing things down so as to avoid our own extinction, we can map out a series of concrete, practical steps we can take that are feasible in the short term—technologically, economically, politically, and psychologically.

We can't expect to transform human nature and convince everyone to change their water-abusing behaviors overnight. People don't want to pay more for water. They don't want to dramatically reduce their usage. They like their top-loading washing machines and their green lawns. They worry that environmental regulation will hurt economic development. They'd rather shell out for Aquafina than for an upgraded water treatment plant. And they find the idea of recycling wastewater from drains and sewers gross rather than practical.

But we can change minds when we have to. Every time a news story pops up about a drought-stricken town left with only a few days' water supply, the notion of recycled water seems a little less radical. Every time a water main explodes, people start to think about the wisdom of replacing the ancient pipes leaking beneath their own city streets. The question is whether we will address our problems smartly and voluntarily, or whether we will wait until a crisis forces us to do so. The former is much less costly and painful.

For a while, I was thinking we should call the film *A River in Egypt,* since so many of us are in a state of denial about the water problem. But that's not quite right, because "denial" implies that there is a problem one is aware of and that one chooses to ignore. I think what we have in the United States is not denial, but ignorance of the problem. As long as the water flows out of our taps, it's hard for us to notice that anything is amiss.

But once people learn about the problem, I do believe we'll see progress. Many times when discussing the project with "outsiders," I would be asked, "So what's the solution?"—as though there were one magic answer that would solve our problems of scarcity, pollution, crumbling infrastructure, and lack of safeguards.

I came across a great line that I've since seen attributed to several people: "There is no silver bullet. Think silver buckshot." The upside of the water crisis is that there is so much room for improvement and so many ways that we can do better, because right now most of us aren't addressing the problem at all. If everyone were motivated to do a little something, it could have a surprisingly great impact.

Silver buckshot. I imagine it looks a little bit like rain.

3

FROM FARMER
TO WATER ACTIVIST

Why I Won't Stop Fighting

Lynn Henning with Kathy Dobie

Lynn Henning has emerged as a leading voice calling on state and federal authorities to hold livestock factory farms accountable to water and air quality laws. With her husband, she farms three hundred acres of corn and soybeans in Lenawee County, Michigan, within ten miles of twelve concentrated animal feeding operation (CAFO) facilities. Concerned over the impact of these CAFOs on local water supplies, Henning helped create the community organization Environmentally Concerned Citizens of South Central Michigan and joined forces with the Sierra Club's Michigan chapter, first as a volunteer water sentinel in 2001 and then as a staff member in 2005.

With the Sierra Club's support, Henning has led efforts to develop water-quality monitoring programs to measure pollution levels from CAFOs and document their impact on local watersheds. Her data and aerial documentation have been used by the Michigan Department of Environmental Quality to better evaluate CAFO permits and levy hundreds of citations for environmental violations. Henning was recognized for her efforts as the North American winner of the 2010 Goldman Environmental Prize.

Kathy Dobie is a freelance writer from Brooklyn, New York, who writes for *GQ, Harper's,* and *O* magazines. She is the author of the memoir *The Only Girl in the Car.*

I'm a family farmer in Lenawee County, Michigan. My husband, Dean, and I grow corn and soybeans on a three hundred–acre farm that has been in his family for four generations. Dean's father is ninety years old, and he's been farming for just over seventy years—his place is right down the road from ours.

Dean and I have been married for thirty-two years. We raised both our children on this farm and our granddaughter comes here now, and she'll ride on the tractor with me or Dean or we'll all take walks in the woods or go fishing in the pond at the back of our property. Over the years we've had lots of family picnics back there and bonfires at night. We grow our own vegetables and do our own canning in the fall, and whatever we don't need, we give away to friends and neighbors.

This was a bucolic, rural area where if somebody got sick, somebody died, we gathered donations, we brought food; we were neighbors. But in the late nineties, our whole way of life changed. That was when factory farms began to come in. They're also called concentrated animal feeding operations or CAFOs, but "factory farm" really fits because they'll keep hundreds, even thousands of animals crowded together in a barn or on an outdoor feedlot—they can't graze or roam or raise their young. If they're kept inside, as they are around here, they stand on cold concrete floors all day, the dairy cows are milked around the clock, sometimes they never even see the outdoors their entire lives. They are nothing more than machines: meat- or milk- or egg-producing machines.

As a family farmer, I'm amazed that the integrity of farming has really gone down the drain. These CAFO owners are not farming for that way of life or to raise food or to be viable to the community. They're there for the money.

We have twelve CAFOs within a ten-mile radius of our farm now. Between them, they house about 20,000 dairy cattle and 10,000 hogs. All of those animals produce millions of gallons of waste—

more waste than the city of Chicago. That waste has to be put some-where. The CAFO operators—I can't call them farmers—use fresh, clean groundwater to wash the waste out of the barns and into giant holding ponds called lagoons. It sits there for weeks and months until it's sprayed or spread onto the fields, where it often runs off into the creeks and rivers and lakes. Right here, in this ten-mile area, we've got over sixty lagoons that can hold up to 400 million gallons of waste. And that's not just manure, urine, and groundwater; it con-tains birthing fluid, blood, hormones, chemicals like ammonia and heavy metals like copper (copper baths are used to clean the cow's hooves), antibiotics put into their feed and antibiotic-resistant bac-teria, pathogens like *E. coli* bacteria, cryptosporidium, and salmo-nella, milk-house wastes, including cleaning agents and bad milk, and silage leachate, which is basically liquid runoff from fermenting fodder—all of it sitting and stewing in these lagoons and then ap-plied to the land over and over and over again.

As you can imagine, the stench is horrible. When they're spread-ing, you can't hang your laundry outside. You can't open your win-dows in the summer. We have infestations of flies and rats. We've got vultures and coyotes because a lot of cows die on these factory farms and the CAFO operators don't always dispose of their bodies properly. Some of the land has been laid so heavily with this manure stew that nothing grows there anymore. So the soil is toxic and the water is polluted. We're seeing the wildlife being affected by what's in the lakes and streams they drink from. We see raccoons wander-ing in the road like they're drunk. We see deer lay down in the ditches because they can't get up and walk.

If anything, the human suffering is even worse. We've got people suffering from asthma and chronic bronchitis, sinus infections and heart problems, and a lot of depression because they can't go outside after they apply the manure, they can't open the windows of their house in warm weather, their children and grandchildren stop visiting because the smell is so awful, they're feeling sick and nauseous all the time, and they can't even sell their homes and leave because their homes aren't worth anything anymore. My father-in-law's farm abuts a CAFO and he and his wife have been diagnosed with hydrogen sulfide poisoning. People feel helpless.

Nobody seems to care. If you're not rich or if you're not in a high-population area, they don't care. You're just collateral damage for the food industry.

The way I got involved in the issue was almost a fluke. In 2000, someone reported a CAFO operator for dumping manure into nearby Lake Hudson. The rumor went around that my husband and I had filed the complaint, even though it wasn't true. I decided to file a Freedom of Information Act request, and I found out that the CAFO next door to us had dumped the manure and another neighbor had called it in. The whole thing made me curious, so Dean and I went over to the lake to have a look, and after that we began to drive around the area to see how many of these factory farms had actually moved in.

We started checking the waterways, and a lot of them looked really sick. You would have water that was tarry black or dirty gray and covered with foam or algae blooms. I grew up around these creeks. We used to play in them when I was a kid. Today you can't do that. You touch the water, you can get sick from all the pathogens that are there. When we were kids, we had catfish, we had pike—and these pike were two, two and a half feet long coming up this creek. We had a ball watching these fish—and now we just have blood worms. And this is all drinking water for people downstream. It's just not right. This guy here can run his waste into a stream that someone else has to drink without knowing it.

That spring I helped start the Environmentally Concerned Citizens of South Central Michigan (ECCSCM). In 2001, I became a volunteer water sentinel for the Michigan chapter of the Sierra Club, and I started monitoring the waterways in the area. In 2005, the Sierra Club put me on staff and began covering the costs of the water testing, but those first few years, Dean and I paid for the equipment and the tests out of our own pockets. I was finding *E. coli* bacteria in the water, and when the state did DNA sampling of the waterways downstream from CAFOs, they discovered cryptosporidium and giardia, which they traced back to the cattle. At one site I tested, I got an *E. coli* count of 7.5 million—Michigan state recommends no body contact with water having an *E. coli* count over three hundred. This was the worst manure discharge I'd ever seen and it took place the day after state agents had conducted an inspection of the facility. It was the CAFO operator's way of saying: You can't tell me what to do. I'll do whatever the hell I want.

At first no one was listening. I would send my results to the Michigan Department of Agriculture and they would say, "Well, that's a Health Department issue." Then when I called the Health Department, they'd say, "You'd better call the Department of Environmental Quality," and then the DEQ would say, "We're not the ones handling that. . . ."

After three years the lightbulb went off, and I said, let's send this to everybody! By that time, we had a system of taking photographs with time and date for credibility. Whenever we took a sample, we took pictures of the sample and pictures of the water where we got the sample. And we started sending our results to *everyone*—the Health Department, the Drain Commission, the Department of Ag, the Department of Natural Resources and Environment, legislators, the governor's office, the state attorney general, the US Environmental Protection Agency—and saying, "This is what's happening right now. Who will respond to this?" And when you send it to everybody, somebody has to jump.

Over the past ten years, state and federal agencies have issued over a thousand citations against these twelve CAFOs for violating such laws as the Clean Water Act. Eleven of the twelve are currently under enforcement or compliance orders by the state. I haven't gotten these results alone—it's been a cooperative effort among the Sierra Club, ECCSCM, and LightHawk, a volunteer environmental aviation organization.

We've come a long way, and where we've gained the most ground is with the aerial photography that we started with LightHawk in 2005. Things were happening in the facilities that we just couldn't see from the ground. But in 2005, a volunteer pilot with LightHawk began taking John Klein, a photographer and a member of ECCSCM, up to shoot pictures of the CAFOs from the air. John takes anywhere from 500 to 2,500 shots, which he later puts onto a disk for me. I examine every single photo—usually at night after Dean has gone to bed. The CAFO operators can get violations from the aerial photos alone, because you can see the hose where the waste is being pumped over into a ditch or the pile of dead animals or the waste from a lagoon overflowing into the calf hutches. It's very visual and very definite.

We pretty much give the agencies all the information they need to issue a violation. I send them the photos or the water test samples with my comments. Basically I'm doing their fieldwork for them. It seems strange, but there are good reasons for it. First off, a lot of our regulatory agencies, the ones responsible for keeping our air and water clean, are underfunded and understaffed. It's very disturbing to me to see the disconnect from reality—people actually think their food supply is protected, when in fact the agencies don't have the funding or the expertise needed to do the inspections. Second, a lot of these agencies have workers who are just there to get a paycheck till they retire. If they're gonna get paid the same amount to sit behind a desk and answer the phone as to go out and climb down in a creek and put cow shit in a bottle, they're not gonna go out if they don't have to.

I'm pretty much self-taught. When the state agency or the feds would come out to do their testing, I would meet them on site so I could observe how they took water samples. Eventually the state wrote a plan laying out the protocols for sampling, and I wrote my own quality assurance plan of my steps and procedures. I wear gloves. I videotape the test. When I take the samples to the treatment plant to be tested, I sign them in. I do everything by the book.

One of the most important things to be able to do is trace the pollution back to its source. These agencies would come out and say, "Yes, we see this creek is polluted with manure runoff, but we don't know the source. So we can't hold anyone accountable." And if they can't hold someone accountable, nothing's going to change. But I was able to trace these discharges back to the source because I know the drainage systems, I know where the tiles are laid (these are porous underground pipes put in originally to drain excess water off the land), I know the individual operations and how they're run. Animal waste can end up in the waterways because it's applied so heavily and the soil is so compacted that the waste simply rolls off the land and into the creeks, especially after it rains. But most often it enters through tiles. So a system that was put in to drain excess water so the farmers could work the land is now basically an underground sewer system, draining animal waste into the waterways.

Operators are not supposed to apply waste before the rain, but all recommended farming practices in Michigan are voluntary since the state passed the Right to Farm Act in 1981. It's enormously clear that self-policing doesn't work, but our legislatures seem unwilling to stand up to powerful business interests, such as the Farm Bureau, and protect the rest of us.

Several times a week I make my rounds, driving about 125 miles each time, checking out the waterways and seeing where the CAFO operators are spreading. Most of them spread waste on land they've leased from other farmers. So I have to be able to track them when they start hauling their waste. I can actually follow their tire marks in the gravel on the road. That way I can find out where a CAFO operator is spreading and see if they're spreading before a predicted rainfall or over an open drainage system or any number of polluting practices. Unlike workers in some agency, I'm here on the ground and my neighbors often are also my eyes and ears. If a CAFO operator is spraying manure out of overhead irrigators in the middle of the night, I'll know about it. A neighbor will call, and then Dean and I will hop in the car and go on what we call "midnight poop runs."

We had some reporters from the *Detroit Free Press* come down here one day, and I took them out to a field where these guys were spreading liquid and then solid waste, and one reporter was saying, "Oh, that smells nasty!" We were on a dirt road and there wasn't any traffic coming, so I stopped the car. She started yelling, "Oh, you can't stop! Oh my God, that smell! We're gonna die! Get us out of here!"

I said, "No, this is what we have to live with and you need to understand that. You live in the city, but we live here. We have to work outside. We're farmers. We're trapped in it. You're eating that smell. It's in your lungs. It's in your nose. You will smell that for hours if you don't go home and wash your nose. It's like you can't get it off of you." We can't even go out in the garden on some days because it's so bad. One time when they spread across from our house, they hauled in tons and tons and tons of waste and stockpiled it right across the road. We couldn't open the windows for two weeks. In August. With no air conditioning. My granddaughter could not even come to the house.

When you can't even have family at your house, it's very degrading. It feels like you've become lowlifes; your family can't even visit. It's humiliating that your community has been let down and taken over.

An elderly couple called me once because their well had become contaminated. They told me they were considering suicide because they couldn't go outside, they couldn't open their windows, they had to wear face masks—they were directly across from a CAFO and they got these emissions every day. Their children wouldn't come see them at all and they couldn't even sell their house because it wasn't worth anything anymore. They felt they were worth more dead than they were alive.

This is the level of powerlessness people feel here. And they're afraid to complain. It's mostly an elderly population and they're afraid of being bullied and harassed by the CAFO owners. One CAFO operator signed a paper saying he wouldn't spread outside a house where a teenage girl with asthma lives. The mother begged the owner and he promised to stop. He even signed an agreement, then just went right on spreading.

They've harassed me and my family. They've left dead animals on our front porch, stuffed in our mailbox, and draped over our vehicles. We've had our mailbox blown up. Our combine has been damaged. Someone shot out a window in my son's house one night—it was the window of the bedroom where my granddaughter was sleeping. I've been called a white-haired witch, a terrorist, Osama bin Laden.

One afternoon while I was out monitoring the water, two manure haulers tried to run me off the road. One was coming right down the center of the road toward me and another was barreling behind me. Luckily I was able to pull into somebody's driveway. But then they blocked the drive so I couldn't get out.

The owner of the CAFO arrived in his pickup truck and they called the state police. When the officer got there, he told me he was going to have to charge me with reckless driving. "I've got three witnesses," he said.

"Really?" I said, and then I pulled my camera out and I started showing him still pictures of the manure tractor-trailer coming at me head-on, and he said, "You're free to go, Mrs. Henning. We will take care of this." I figured if I was going to die that day at least some-body would have pictures of who did it.

After Dean retired from Ford Motor Company in 2005, he began to accompany me on all my rounds. He had worked at Ford for thirty-two years while farming full-time. Now we work side by side. I help him farm and he helps me do my water monitoring. While I get my water samples, he stays by the car and keeps an eye out on the road to see if anyone's coming who might cause problems. He keeps the motor running and I leave my car door open so if we need to, we can get out of there fast.

One day a CAFO operator started chasing us down the road in his truck. He stayed right on us. While Dean drove, I called the sher-iff's department and told them we had been out monitoring the water and now we had a pickup truck tailing us. They told me to drive straight to the sheriff's department and so we raced into town and when we got there, it was right out of a movie—the officers were out of their cars with their guns over the roofs. After we got out of our car, the CAFO operator tried to take a swing at me, but an officer grabbed him and told him he would go to jail if he touched me. I can't be intimidated, but a lot of the people here, understandably, are afraid to speak out.

In 2010, I was awarded the Goldman Environmental Prize for my work exposing the polluting practices of factory farms. It was a great honor. People call me a fighter, but I don't see it that way. I look at what I do as holding up the mirror and saying: This is what is going on. This needs to be changed. You're not being told the truth about where your food comes from.

This is affecting people across the country and across the world, and it's huge because this is our food supply, our water, our air, and our land. And being a farmer, I think it's my obligation to help ed-ucate people on what's really happening out here.

I'm a documentarian. A mirror holder. As a farmer, I know how irrigation and drainage systems work, how a field is supposed to look, the right way to grow healthy food and treat your animals. I know how to do research—I use aerial photography, satellite imagery, GPS coordinates, the Freedom of Information Act, whatever tools are out there.

And I won't give up. They wish I would, but I'll never go away.

4

CLEAN WATER—
THE PRICE OF GOLD?

Resource Development and
Global Competition for Water

Robert Moran

Robert Moran of Michael-Moran Associates, LLC, has forty years' experience in conducting and managing water-quality, geochemical, and hydrogeologic work for private investors, industrial clients, tribal and citizens groups, NGOs, law firms, and governmental agencies at all levels. Much of his technical expertise involves the quality and geochemistry of natural and contaminated waters and sediments as related to mining, nuclear fuel cycle sites, industrial development, geothermal resources, hazardous wastes, and water supply development. In addition, Moran has significant experience in the application of remote sensing to natural resource issues, development of resource policy, and litigation support. He has worked on hydrogeologic issues in countries ranging from Australia, Greece, Mali, and Gambia to Mongolia, Colombia, Belgium, Great Britain, and the United States. He has a PhD in geological sciences from the University of Texas at Austin.

If you mention the world water crisis to the average informed American, several images are likely to come to mind: the parched

American Southwest, with the glittering, fast-growing city of Las Vegas at its heart, using dwindling water resources to water golf courses and feed fountain displays in front of casinos; the expanding Sahara Desert in northern Africa, creating flights of refugees from drought-stricken, famine-plagued lands no longer able to support agriculture; and perhaps the melting ice packs in the Arctic, where global climate change is transforming some of the world's largest remaining reserves of freshwater into rising levels of salty oceanic tides.

It's unlikely that most people think of one of the world's largest gold mines, hidden in a remote mountain range in a central Asian country few Americans could locate on a map. Yet that is one of the most recent water crisis hot spots I've visited in my work as a consulting hydrogeologist. It's a potent symbol of how great-power geopolitics, corporate thirst for profits, governmental corruption, and above all the corrosive power of secrecy are combining to intensify water-use problems in dozens of locations around the world—with disturbing long-term implications for all of us.

The mine is the Kumtor Mine, owned and operated by the Canadian company Centerra Gold, through its subsidiaries, Kumtor Gold Company CJSC and the Kumtor Operating Company. The country is Kyrgyzstan (officially the Kyrgyz Republic), a former Soviet republic, whose government owns roughly one-third of Centerra by way of Kyrgyzaltyn JSC, a state-owned entity. Between 1996 and the end of 2010, the Kumtor mine produced 7.8 million ounces of gold, an amount that makes it one of the ten richest gold mines on earth.

The Kumtor mine is located high in the Tien Shan mountains, close to the Chinese border. But although it is remote, the Kumtor mine looms large in the economy of Kyrgyzstan. The country is extremely poor, with only a few exportable resources capable of generating desperately needed foreign exchange income. Two of the most important of those resources are metals (including gold, silver,

and uranium, rare earth elements—used extensively in modern alternative energy applications), and other specialized minerals used
in high-tech manufacturing) and water used to generate power. In
the Tien Shan region, all of these resources come together.

The Kumtor mine produces gold, silver, and reportedly other
elements; as we'll see, much of the mine's operations are shrouded
in secrecy, so no one outside of a few business leaders and perhaps
some government insiders really knows for sure the complete list
of resources being extracted from the mountains. At least 7 percent
of Kyrgyzstan's gross domestic product is generated by the Kumtor
mine, along with one-third of its exports. And although the region
is largely arid, its high elevation and numerous glaciers create rivers
whose waters can be dammed to produce electricity—though global
climate change has already begun melting those glaciers. So what
happens in and around the Kumtor mine has an enormous impact
on the economics of Kyrgyzstan and the future of its people.

In September 2011, I traveled to Kyrgyzstan to visit the Kumtor
mine. I'd been invited by Erkingül Imankodjoeva, a member of the
national parliament, as well as by a Kyrgyz nongovernmental organization (NGO) known as the Human Development Center (HDC)
Tree of Life. The trip would be paid for by CEE Bankwatch, an independent organization that monitors projects funded by European
banks to determine their environmental and social impacts. (The
mine's operations have been funded largely through subsidized loans
from the European Bank for Reconstruction and Development,
which is supposed to support only projects that produce major economic benefits to the countries in which they're located.)

I'd been asked to serve on an official Kyrgyz government commission team charged with studying and reporting on the operations
of the mine. The commission members included Kalia Moldogazieva, a physician, environmental scientist, and director of HDC
Tree of Life, a couple of other NGO representatives, some Kyrgyz

scientists who had worked with Centerra and were familiar with the mine site, and a German documentary filmmaker who would record our visit.

The final commissioner was Imankodjoeva herself, who represents the mountain village where in 1998 a major environmental disaster occurred. A truck delivering sodium cyanide—a chemical used in mineral processing—to the Kumtor mine plunged into the Barksoon River, a local source of drinking water. It spilled nearly two tons of cyanide, causing the deaths of at least four people and sickness in many more due to cyanide poisoning. As a member of parliament, Imankodjoeva has an obvious personal and political interest in monitoring the operations of the mine—and in fact she is still battling, along with local residents, to uncover fuller information about the 1998 accident and arrange appropriate financial compensation for those who were harmed.

The commission's mandate was to study several facets of the mine's operations, including whether its workers are being treated humanely. My focus, of course, would be on water-related issues. From my previous work in Kyrgyzstan, it became very clear why a special commission to investigate the Kumtor mine was necessary. Few outside travelers visit this portion of the Tien Shan mountains, which loom up to 26,000 feet over a desolate region of Kyrgyzstan just forty kilometers from the Chinese border—with the exception of narcotics traffickers who reportedly use the local passes. The mine itself is above 14,000 feet in elevation, and the nearest village (other than the complex of specially built workers' housing) is more than one hundred kilometers away. For all practical purposes, it's a secret facility; the company managers and government officials on site can say anything they want about what's happening there, with little chance of being contradicted by any independent source of information. In 2008, Czech filmmaker Tomas Kudra obtained permission to make a documentary film titled *All That Glitters,* showing

Kumtor operations. However, the Kumtor Operating Company apparently considered the film too controversial, and it has never officially been shown in Kyrgyzstan.

For these reasons, a handful of Kyrgyz political leaders and local and international NGOs had long been pressuring the government to mount an official investigation into the workings at Kumtor. Demonstrations during the first three months of 2011 by local residents convinced that Kumtor's operations were damaging the environment added fuel to the fire. I skeptically wondered whether the Kyrgyz government might also have desired ammunition to extract additional financial concessions from the Canadian operating company or even perhaps to force nationalization of the operations. Whatever the combination of reasons, the commission was finally formed, and I was named a member. But the formation of the commission didn't mark the end of attempts to deflect attention from the Kumtor story.

In August 2011 the NGO activists appeared to receive approval from the Kyrgyz government for a team of eight commissioners, including me, to enter the Kumtor mine site and conduct a thorough audit. I got a call from my sponsors at HDC Tree of Life, saying, "Please get on a plane and come to Kyrgyzstan."

The flight from my home near Denver via Istanbul to Bishkek was long and exhausting. We immediately began by reviewing the available company data and reports. I interviewed the other technical members of the commission team and investigated the competence of several government analytical laboratories—a touchy task given that the government is part owner of the mine. But within a few days of my arrival, I got word that the president of Kumtor Gold had told the prime minister of Kyrgyzstan, in effect, "The commission can visit the mine at a date we'll announce shortly. But there's one member we can't allow on site—and that is Robert Moran." At least Kumtor was being consistent about my access to the mine. During both of my visits in 1999, the Soros Foundation had requested that I be allowed to visit the mine. In both cases, the requests were rejected or ignored.

It's not a coincidence that I was excluded, since I was the only member of the independent commission with applied technical expertise in evaluating mining-water operations and impacts, and was not Kyrgyz. Kumtor and similar operations often supply tours to average citizens and officials for public relations purposes, but seldom to experts they don't control, financially or otherwise.

Clearly Kumtor Gold's commitment to transparency on water and environmental matters appears shallow at best.

Nonetheless, having flown so far to shed light on these issues, I pressed ahead. While ensconced in a walled hotel compound on the edge of Bishkek, with security cameras everywhere, I studied the available documents and quickly prepared a sampling program and instructions to direct Moldogazieva on how she should collect samples and make water-quality measurements. Despite the company's rejection, we decided that I would unofficially visit the margins of the mine on horseback to observe the facilities and make field water-quality measurements.

Along with some of the other commissioners, I traveled to the villages of Barskoon and Tamga, high in the mountains about one hundred kilometers from the mine, which would be the staging area for the commission's work. Our group drove by car from Barskoon and joined some local Kyrgyz who had transported sturdy central-Asian horses to within a few kilometers of the mine boundary. Then, guided by the former head of Kumtor security—who had also been a soldier for the Kyrgyz-Soviet military in Afghanistan in 1980 and 1981—the film journalist and I ventured as close as possible to the edge of the mine property on horseback, carrying portable scientific and film gear. Riding around the margins of the mine, we filmed everything we could and made water-quality measurements from the surface waters up-gradient of the mine and at the Kumtor River, which flows through the mine, where it leaves the mine facilities.

While the other commissioners toured the facility, I did my best to observe the property from its perimeter, despite my exclusion from the mine itself. I used the field information together with the water analyses we subsequently received to write a report on water issues and other environmental problems at the mine, which were shared with the other commission members in the fall of 2011.

What I found confirmed the suspicions of environmental experts around the world. The Kumtor mine uses and contaminates tremendous volumes of water, seriously reduces fish populations, reduces and degrades water needed from vital purposes including agriculture and human consumption, and aggravates the destruction of glaciers that is already being accelerated by global climate change. Even the lake Kumtor uses (fed by glacial meltwaters) for its drinking water is being contaminated by the metal-laden dust and other wastes the mine activities generate.

To understand why the Kumtor mine has such a damaging impact on local water supplies, one needs to know a bit about how gold and silver are mined and processed in remote regions like Kyrgyzstan.

The mining techniques used at sites such as Kumtor are simple, aggressive, and economically efficient. First, workers use explosives and heavy mechanical equipment to remove the uneconomic waste rock covering the mineralized, valuable ore. At Kumtor, for many years the waste rock was placed on top of the nearby glaciers, due to space limitations. In some locations, the glaciers themselves were actually mined out to gain access to the valuable ores. Again, explosives are used to fragment the mineralized rock, sometimes removing the tops of mountains. The fragmented ore is taken out and transported to a processing plant using immense earthmoving machines. This is done in stages, ultimately resulting in a huge pit. (At Kumtor the main pit was 842 meters deep, and two accessory pits were 365 meters deep.) The formerly buried, fragmented rock—both the ores and waste rock—contains high concentrations of many different metals, other chemical components, and blasting residues, some of them toxic. Soon groundwater begins to flow into the pit, along with meltwater from the nearby glaciers, and chemically reacts with the rock, mobilizing the contaminants.

To allow mine workers and heavy equipment to work in the pit, all this accumulated water must be pumped out into the surrounding environment. Of course, all kinds of materials dissolved or suspended in the water, many of them potentially toxic, are pumped into the environment along with the water.

This is just the start of the pollution caused by mining and associated processing. Once the mine workers transport the rock to the nearby processing plant, it is crushed up and mixed with massive quantities of chemicals. All of this matter is moved in and out of the plant in the form of a slurry mixed with water (tailings). The amounts of water required are gigantic: an estimated 4.38 billion liters of water per year are extracted from local sources for use in the Kumtor mine.

The impacts of this vast water use are huge and complicated. There is literally no way of utilizing it without creating significant environmental impacts. If one takes the water for the mineral processing from these headwaters, others downstream are prevented from using that water—for example, local farmers, sheep herders, or villagers who have relied on that river for generations to nurture their crops and animals as well as for washing and personal consumption. By the time the water is returned to the environment after the processing is completed, it is contaminated with many pollutants, including rock contaminants (such as arsenic, copper, zinc, nickel, and uranium), explosives, fuels, oils, grease, antifreeze, sewage waste, and residual forms of cyanide used in gold and silver extraction. In fact, the amount of cyanide used at Kumtor is between eight and ten tons *per day*—and that's according to a spokesman for the mine, which means it may be understated. Finally, much of the process water is lost via heating and evaporation, dramatically reducing the amount of water in the system for living things, including local humans, to use.

One must understand that the mine wastes (the waste rock and tailings) will remain on the site forever—not a thousand years or a million years, but forever. And the site will require perpetual maintenance. This is far from trivial, as the climate and weathering in the Tien Shan are extreme and the region is subject to frequent, strong earthquakes. Previous expert reports have already shown that the waste rock piles, tailings impoundment, and glacial dam holding back the water supply lake are unstable, moving downhill, and liable to catastrophic collapse. Any such event would increase the already significant water contamination.

It would be very useful to be able to track how water use and other activities at the Kumtor mine have been affecting the local and downstream environments over the past two decades. What are the loads of contaminants being carried downstream in pounds or kilograms per day? It would also be helpful to know how Kumtor's impact on the environment has changed over time—especially because the affected river eventually flows into neighboring Uzbekistan, a traditional resource and political rival for Kyrgyzstan. Unfortunately, it's difficult even to make precise estimates about these trends because of the secrecy surrounding Kumtor's operations. As I wrote in my report, "Kumtor Operating Company (KOC) controls the collection and flow of essentially all of the project-related information (environmental, social, investment, etc.) to the public and regulators. KOC pays for and directs the collection and distribution of all project technical information. Truly independent environmental and social information is not available."

How typical is this Kumtor situation? Increasingly around the world, mines are located in physically isolated areas, not simply because "that is where the minerals are," but because the overall impacts are perceived to be politically unacceptable in populated areas. Imagine the public furor that would develop if a company proposed operating a huge open-pit mine near Paris, London, or New York City.

In countries such as Canada and the United States, and regions such as Western Europe, mine operators contract to have environmental impact studies prepared, as well as detailed technical reports on hydrogeology, water quality, aquifer and pit inflow impacts, geochemistry, socioeconomic impacts, feasibility (ore treatability) studies, and so on. The environmental impact studies are routinely made public, but regulators, the public, and researchers may be unaware that more detailed reports have also been prepared, and they often fail to request copies of them. These are the sources of the real details. If the public does request copies, they are often made public. But not in Kyrgyzstan, and not in many developing countries. What's more, some of the most important studies of the Kumtor mine—conducted by company employees rather than independent experts—were written in English and never translated into the two main languages of Kyrgyzstan, Kyrgyz and Russian. This limits their accessibility and usefulness to local lawmakers, policy advocates, NGOs, and ordinary citizens. Given the international patterns, this approach seems deliberate.

In hindsight, it seemed that the Kumtor officials were putting every possible impediment in the path of the commission team's attempts to collect water quality samples and field measurements. These disruptive efforts included excluding me from the mine; creating unreasonable "confusions" regarding the dates and times of the site visit; and delaying all later efforts so that inadequate daylight was available for complete sampling. Strangely, some of the water samples failed to arrive at the Central Laboratory with the others, and inexplicably arrived a day later. When we finally tabulated the laboratory data, it became clear that many metals were missing from the analysis of the most downstream site—the site that presents the clearest picture of which contaminants were leaving the mine site and flowing downstream. Finally, although the company collected their own water quality samples on September 20, 2011, none of these results have been released to the commission team or the public. Had Kumtor been truly interested in openness and transparency, they could have facilitated the commission's tasks; instead they impeded them at every opportunity.

It's too soon to tell whether the commission report to which I contributed in 2011 will become widely available to the regulators and people of Kyrgyzstan, or whether it will affect the future of the Kumtor mine.

For the people of Kyrgyzstan, it's a tragic setback to their efforts to obtain open information about a project that affects their lives and their country. But why should the rest of us be concerned? There are several reasons.

First, initial funding for these water and resource projects comes largely from multilateral lending institutions, such as the European Bank for Reconstruction and Development (EBRD) and the World Bank, which are based in the developed world and are largely controlled by and heavily funded by taxpayer funds from developed countries. In a very real sense, the Kumtor mine was built with our money. The original mission of the EBRD was to assist the countries of the formerly communist bloc in building their private sectors. Headquartered in London, the EBRD is now owned by sixty-one countries and two international institutions, with both the United States and the UK serving as funding members. Most projects supported by EBRD are, like Kumtor, privately owned and managed for profit—which raises the question as to whether supporting businesses that may be enriching shareholders at the expense of local populations and the natural environment is a reasonable use of taxpayer funds.

Second, citizens in developing countries still look to us—the nations of Western Europe, the United States, Canada, Australia, New

Zealand, Scandinavia, and so on—as examples of how international business should be conducted, despite our failings in regard to financial transparency, human rights abuses, and sustainable environmental practices. Unfortunately, we also have taken the lead in promoting practices that have weakened government enforcement of water, auditing, and resource-related laws, and promoted self-regulation by industry—and the developing world has been watching and copying these practices. Our collective reputations are at stake and in many instances have been badly damaged. Despite repeated promises, too often our international corporations operate overseas in ways that would not be tolerated at home.

Third, pragmatically, it is in our self-interest to prevent or minimize water and resource disputes in these conflict areas. Fifty years ago, resource stability in central Asia may not have mattered much to the United States or Europe; that is no longer true.

I've now been to Kyrgyzstan three times in the past twelve years, and I've witnessed a polarization and hardening of attitudes. I was always impressed with the general tolerance for cultural and religious differences in this nominally Muslim country. Now, however, political, ethnic, and religious differences have been magnified by the world economic crisis. Since the collapse of the Soviet Union in 1991, corruption has increased such that in 2010, Transparency International's Corruption Perception Index ranked Kyrgyzstan at 164th out of 178 countries, equal with the Democratic Republic of Congo, Guinea, and Venezuela. Now this tiny country of about 5.5 million inhabitants is being pressured by three of the major world powers—Russia, China, and the United States. All three countries want to influence the Kyrgyz business, military, and resource decisions.

The US government operates the Manas air base outside Bishkek, which is a staging location for military deployments in central Asia, especially Afghanistan, for which it pays a fee on the order of $65 million a year. That fee was significantly increased in the last set of negotiations due to pressure from the Russian government, which still has its own sphere of influence throughout the former Soviet republics. In fact, many of the Kyrgyz borders are still patrolled by Russian, not Kyrgyz troops.

Because it is a former Soviet republic, the dominant business language of Kyrgyzstan is still Russian, and it represents a market for Russia's goods. In addition, it is a buffer zone separating Russia from the instability of the more radical Muslim states to the south and from the influence of the United States in central Asia.

The Chinese are the third player in today's three-sided battle for influence. Many of Kyrgyzstan's trade connections have traditionally run through the mountain passes that connect the country with China. Today almost all the explosives and many of the processing chemicals used at the Kumtor mine are bought from China. Furthermore, the Chinese themselves are becoming an increasing presence in Kyrgyzstan as part of their global campaign to increase access to the natural resources their rapidly growing economy needs. Numerous mines similar to the Kumtor facility are being proposed for operation all over Kyrgyzstan under Chinese auspices. Judging by the low levels of environmental protection prevalent in China itself, one can only assume that the depredations being practiced by these Chinese operations are likely to be even worse than those found at Kumtor. Finally, much of neighboring China is desert or semi-desert, which means that China naturally covets some of the Kyrgyz water.

Questionable governance practices are especially apparent in a case like the Kumtor mine, which is owned in part by the Kyrgyz government and in which individual officials of the Kyrgyzstan government are said to hold unknown numbers of additional shares. No one with real power has any serious incentive to curb the environmental damage occurring at Kumtor. So the problems at Kumtor, far from being purely local, are linked to great power rivalries as well as economic and political entanglements that involve all of us. And the location of the Kumtor mine creates the potential for serious international conflict over water resources.

The river that flows through the Kumtor mine empties into the Naryn River, one of several in the Tien Shan mountains that flow through a series of countries in the region: Kyrgyzstan, Uzbekistan, Kazakhstan, and China. The three "Stans" are traditionally moderate Muslim regimes that have become radicalized in recent decades. All of these countries are primed for possible hostilities over water.

For example, the Naryn flows from Kyrgyzstan into the Fergana Valley of Uzbekistan, where it joins the Syr Darya, which once flowed into the Aral Sea. Today, however, the river is too depleted to reach the Aral, thanks partly to its use in irrigating cotton fields, and partly to its damming to generate electricity. The Toktogul reservoir alone contains 19.9 cubic kilometers of water that previously would have flowed to the Aral, sustaining farms and communities along its route.

Hydroelectricity dominates Kyrgyzstan's energy balance, providing some two-thirds of the country's electricity. And in the years to come, the country's reliance on water-generated power is expected to increase further. The National Energy Programme of Kyrgyzstan and the Strategy for Fuel and Energy Complex Development both call for the rapid expansion of renewable sources of energy, including the building of some one hundred small hydropower plants along the Naryn and other rivers in eastern Kyrgyzstan.

Today, between irrigation and hydropower, competition for water access is already a major regional issue. That competition is likely to intensify in the years to come. Add to the picture the diversion of water supplies for such projects as the Kumtor mine— and the newer mines being opened throughout the region—and you begin to sense how volatile and potentially explosive water issues may become in the near future. No wonder German diplomat Klaus

Grewlich, in an article examining the challenges facing Afghanistan as it strives for economic and political stability, commented, "The whole Central Asian 'water problem' obviously contains the ingredients for becoming a major socioeconomic and political catastrophe, unless vigorous action leads to expedient and organized change."[1]

———

The Kumtor case is important in its own right, affecting the livelihoods and environment of over 5.5 million people living in Kyrgyzstan as well as the prospects for peace and prosperity through the Central Asia region. But it's also significant as an example of the kinds of problems that affect water usage throughout the world. What lessons can we learn from the story of the Kumtor mine?

First, we need to broaden our perspective on the water issues we face. When we talk about water crises, people think of global climate change, agriculture, and desertification, but they usually don't think about mining and other resource extraction processes that are a huge part of the problem. People think about water conflicts between cities and agricultural users, especially in the developed world, but not about the massive environmental conflicts that are now being engineered in developing countries around the world.

There is a common assumption that we can develop natural resources on a large scale without any significant environmental impacts. We need to lay that myth to rest once and for all. All resource development, whether gold mining, oil or gas exploration, farming, aquaculture, or whatever, involves trade-offs. We need to learn to consider the environmental, social, and economic impacts of every

1 Stratfor Global Intelligence Newsletter, April 8, 2011, www.stratfor.com/other_voices /20110408-kyrgyzstan-regional-water-and-energy-cooperation, accessed December 8, 2011.

development project and ask the hard questions involved: Are these impacts acceptable to the people whose lives are most deeply affected? Who will pay the long-term costs? Who decides?

I once heard one of the founders of modern environmental economics, Herman Daly of the University of Maryland, rail against "one of the greatest myths of modern times, the belief that we can have 'constant growth.'" Of course, he is correct; there are limits to growth. When we ignore those limits, such unhappy episodes as Kumtor are one of the results.

Geographic distance may seem to shield us from these concerns. Most developed countries won't approve or permit grossly harmful developments in or near cities, affluent suburbs, or esthetically attractive areas, such as those favored for tourism. As a result, powerful countries and corporations increasingly are going offshore in search of natural resources, seeking lower operational costs and lax regulation. In essence, underdeveloped countries ranging from Sierra Leone and Papua New Guinea to Bolivia and—yes—Kyrgyzstan are becoming "resource colonies," treated almost as private fiefdoms for the benefit of owners and their allies in government.

Kumtor also offers us a warning about the dangers of giving corporations unfettered control not only over natural resources but also over information about their activities.

As the Kumtor story suggests, natural resource development usually requires tremendous volumes of water, with environmental effects that can be national, international, and even global in scope. Yet in much of the world, national governments permit international corporations to extract, use, consume, and pollute this water at *no* cost for the commodity itself. (This appears to be the case in Kyrgyzstan; as best as I can determine, the operators of the Kumtor mine pay nothing to the government or to the affected communities for the vast volumes of water they use.) In some cases, corporations are charged for using surface water (from rivers, streams, lakes, and reservoirs) but can extract groundwater free of charge. This often leads to perverse approaches, with companies constructing extraction wells around the perimeter of high-elevation lakes to avoid siphoning water out of the lakes directly. Traditional cost-benefit analyses are largely useless when it comes to evaluating the utility of mining water impacts, as they generally disregard the cost of the water itself, and the real cost of cleaning the contaminated water.

Furthermore, in both developed and undeveloped countries, much water infrastructure (such as canals, dams, aqueducts, reservoirs, levees, water treatment plants, and so on) is paid for by taxpayers. In many cases, industries from agribusiness to manufacturing to resource extraction are permitted to use this infrastructure without payment, a form of indirect subsidy that reduces the costs of goods, encourages waste, and prevents the discovery of a true market price for one of the most precious commodities in the world: water.

What's more, we've even permitted *information* about water supply, use, consumption, and pollution to be privatized. As I've discovered in my work as a hydrogeologist, the flow of information about water and water-use projects to concerned NGOs and the general public is severely restricted. Most project-related data is collected by the company or its paid consultants, which means that the information selectively released to the public and to regulators and policy makers is often untrustworthy, and much of it is little better than propaganda.

Recent trends have worsened all of the problems I've just described. The fall of the Soviet empire and the global victory of capitalism brought many benefits to humankind, but triumphalism on the political Right has brought with it a tendency to demonize government, disparage the importance of regulation, and assume that the private sector is *always* more efficient, productive, and creative than the public sector. As a result, there has been a growing readiness to privatize major development projects, including those that profoundly impact water resources, from mining and oil drilling to dams and water utilities.

With governments around the world increasingly strapped for staff and funding, public oversight of these privatized water enterprises has diminished, leaving businesses free to exploit for private benefit the natural resources that should be the common inheritance of humanity. Finally, weak economic conditions around the world in the wake of the 2008–2009 recession have further impoverished governments, increased the degree of competition for natural resources, and heightened the pressure on countries and regions to make their "business climates" more attractive through lower taxes and further gutting of regulations. Even where the laws governing resource development are strict—and there are reams of such laws at both the national and international levels—enforcement ranges from inconsistent to negligible, especially in poorly developed countries. Across much of the planet, minimal oversight combined with government corruption is the norm.

It's no wonder, then, that we see the Kumtor story being repeated, with variations, in many places around the world. We see it in the Atacama Desert in Chile, an arid region with virtually no recorded rainfall where tremendous volumes of much-needed water are being diverted to extract and process copper ores. We see it in Johannesburg, South Africa, where long-standing gold mining operations have contaminated the groundwater under much of the city. We see it in Papua New Guinea, where an operation run by the state mining company of China is using up freshwater in the development of copper, nickel, and other metals, then risking damage to the coral reefs and marine ecosystem by dumping the mine wastes into the ocean via a pipeline. We see it in Iraq, where the Tigris and Euphrates Rivers, the historic cradle of civilization, are being contaminated as a by-product of oil and gas development and warfare. We see it in Bolivia, where water extracted from high desert *salars* (salt flats) is being used for the extraction of silver and other metals, depriving alpaca herders and quinoa growers of the water they need.

If we don't act soon to respond to the warning that the story of Kumtor mine provides, we may find the dangers it represents on our very doorstep.

On departing Bishkek, I was informed that the Kyrgyz KGB—that is, the secret police—wished to read my draft report. Apparently the KGB was brought into these activities as a way to "shelter" some commission members from undue outside pressures—immediately before the first open presidential election in Kyrgyzstan's history. This isn't the kind of transparency and accountability I'd hoped to see at Kumtor—or the kind of governance system needed in Kyrgyzstan. Unfortunately, it is all too typical of water and natural resource governance in many developing countries.

5

NO TIME TO WASTE

Alex Prud'homme

Alex Prud'homme has been a professional writer for twenty years. He has written about a wide range of subjects for the *New York Times,* the *New Yorker, Vanity Fair, Talk,* and *Time.* His books include *Forewarned,* with Michael Cherkasky, about terrorism and security; *The Cell Game,* about the ImClone scandal and biotech; and *My Life in France,* with Julia Child, a best-selling memoir about how Julia learned to cook in Paris (on which half of *Julie & Julia,* the Nora Ephron movie starring Meryl Streep, was based).

In June 2011, Scribner published Prud'homme's latest book, *The Ripple Effect: The Fate of Freshwater in the Twenty-First Century,* which inspired Participant Media's documentary film *Last Call at the Oasis.*

The Ripple Effect is about how freshwater will become the defining resource of our time—"the next oil." The book explores water challenges, from disputes over pollutants, bottled water, and energy to privatization and sustainability, and solutions, such as new treatment and conservation technologies, and the growing public dialogue over the value of water. Prud'homme has discussed the book on *The Daily Show with Jon Stewart* and with Don Imus on *Imus in the Morning,* and has written about flood, drought, water pollution, and levees for the *New York Times.*

Prud'homme lives with his wife and two children in Brooklyn, New York.

"THE STORY OF THE CENTURY"

A few years ago, a globe-trotting hydrogeologist named Robert Moran told me that water is the key resource that underlies every other one. As the population grows, diets change, people choose to live in deserts or floodplains, and the climate heats up, he said, we no longer will be able to take supplies of plentiful, clean water for granted. "For better or worse," Moran added, "freshwater is the story of the century."

It was a statement that took me by surprise at first, but the more I thought about it the more sense it made. Growing crops, building homes, fabricating computer chips, generating electricity, mining for gold, and drilling for oil all require copious amounts of H_2O. And although it's true that oil dominated geopolitics in the last century, that was an aberration: for most of history, water has been the most critical resource. After all, you can live without oil (with difficulty, to be sure), but you cannot survive without freshwater. As I researched the subject, I became convinced that water will reassert itself as the critical resource of the twenty-first century.

The idea seemed fascinating, and more than a little worrying, and I thought water would make a good subject for an article. But as I began to talk to experts, I realized that water—a clear, nearly tasteless, seemingly simple resource—is actually a vastly complex, constantly evolving, emotionally charged subject. If I really wanted to understand what Moran meant, I would have to forget the article and write a book instead.

So I followed the story. Starting in 2007, I embarked on what I figured would be a one- or two-year project. I traveled up to Poland Springs, Maine, to learn about the debate over bottled water; down to the Chesapeake Bay, where man-made dead zones are destroying one of the richest aquasystems on earth; visited the levees that failed New Orleans in Hurricane Katrina; toured desert-bound Las Vegas and its draining reservoir, Lake Mead; interviewed the billionaire T. Boone Pickens in Dallas about his plan to sell water from the Ogallala Aquifer; inspected the San Francisco Bay Delta, where a "megaflood" could wipe out much of California's freshwater supply;

and investigated a resource war in Alaska that pits the world's last pristine sockeye salmon fishery against what could be the nation's largest copper mine. It was a thrilling, shocking, and enlightening series of experiences.

As I pieced the book together, the biggest challenges were deciding what to leave out and how to present the information in a way that made sense. Ultimately the book I produced, *The Ripple Effect,* took more than three years to write. It was published in June 2011 and inspired the film *Last Call at the Oasis.*

From my perspective, the movie is evidence that water awareness has begun to enter our collective consciousness for the first time since the environmental movement of the late 1960s and the signing of the Clean Water Act in 1972 (itself instigated, in part, by events such as the spontaneous combustion of the Cuyahoga River and the poisonings in Love Canal). The film also signifies that today's conservationists—energized by the sinking of the *Deepwater Horizon* offshore drilling rig, the battle over mountaintop coal mining, the debate over hydrofracking for natural gas, and the protest against the Keystone XL Pipeline from Alberta, Canada, to the Gulf of Mexico—have started a vibrant dialogue about how we will use and value water in coming decades. My hope is that the film, and this book, will expand and amplify that conversation, for our water supplies are in deepening trouble.

WHAT I FOUND: BLACK MAYONNAISE, GROUND ZERO, AND THE MAN WITH THE TOOTHBRUSH

In America, we are hydrologically blessed: we can turn the tap on at any time of day and get some of the cleanest H_2O in the world, at whatever temperature we want, for as long as we want, at hardly any cost. We have gotten so good at collecting, treating, and transporting water that it seems limitless, and therefore unimportant. We don't think twice about gulping down a tall glass of cool, clean water on a hot summer day—as much of the developing world does. (Over a billion people worldwide lack clean drinking supplies, and over 2 billion lack adequate sanitation, which leads to disease and death.) But as I looked a little closer, I discovered that the quality and quantity of American water has undergone staggering changes lately, mostly out of the public eye.

Although the United States is using water more efficiently than ever now—thanks largely to industry's attempt to cut down on cost and improve efficiency—it is clear that most Americans don't have a clue about how we use water. Nearly forty years after the signing of the Clean Water Act (CWA), our water supplies are becoming more, not less, polluted. Between 2004 and 2009, the CWA was violated at least 506,000 times by more than 23,000 companies, according to data from the federal Environmental Protection Agency (EPA) reviewed by the *New York Times*. And during that same period, tap water was contaminated by 316 different pollutants in forty-five states, according to the Environmental Working Group. Every year, seven hundred new chemicals reach the marketplace, yet few of them are tested for toxicity, and many will end up in the water supply. Our waters are filled with new kinds of pollution, but we also have plenty of old "legacy" pollutants, as I discovered in my own backyard.

In Newtown Creek—about a mile and a half from my house in Brooklyn, New York—one of the largest oil spills in history has been seeping into the water and soil of the Greenpoint neighborhood for over a century. The lake of viscous, toxic goop that pollutes Newtown Creek, known as "black mayonnaise," is far larger than the infamous *Exxon Valdez* spill in Alaska, and the oil spills that coated New Orleans during Hurricane Katrina. Until the *Deepwater Horizon* sank in 2010, it was the largest oil spill in US history. The spill sits in the heart of the most densely populated metropolis in the country, it has contaminated a deep aquifer, and there are unusual cancer clusters nearby. Yet hardly anyone knows about it, even today, because it was covered up and not cleaned up. (The EPA finally named Newtown Creek a Superfund site in late 2010. This means it is one of the most polluted waterways in the nation, slated for a thorough cleanup funded by the polluters and the federal government, but it will take decades to accomplish this, and even then the site won't be completely remediated, thanks to overflowing sewers.)

I was equally disturbed to discover that New York, and indeed much of the United States, is unprepared for the floods and droughts predicted to come with climate change. Global warming will raise sea levels, put more water vapor into the atmosphere, and create more frequent and violent storms. Yet much of our critical infrastructure—highways, airports, train tracks, sewage treatment plants, and the like—is at or below sea level, and we have hardly any meaningful flood defenses.

In New Orleans the US Army Corps of Engineers is rebuilding the same kinds of levees that failed during Hurricane Katrina, at a cost of hundreds of millions of dollars. In the Midwest floods along the Mississippi have caused billions of dollars of damage. In the San Francisco Bay delta, an earthquake zone, the levees are a century old and leaking, but political gridlock has stymied improvements: Sacramento, rich farmland, endangered species, and the majority of California's freshwater supply are at grave risk. California is now the eighth-largest economy in the world: if the San Francisco delta were to flood with seawater, the consequences would dwarf the impact of Katrina. Meanwhile, the nation's East Coast is statistically due for a major hurricane, but people refuse to take the threat seriously, and storm defenses are poor or nonexistent.

We are equally ill-equipped for drought. Although it might seem obvious that a place like Las Vegas (the driest city in the nation) or

Phoenix (the hottest city in the nation)—both in Ground Zero for global warming—are unprepared for more arid conditions, the same is true for cities such as New York, Boston, Philadelphia, Washington, D.C., or Atlanta. This was made vivid to me on the day I dropped six hundred feet beneath Manhattan, into New York City's new Water Tunnel Number 3, which the city is building as fast as possible because Tunnels 1 and 2 are so old they are on the verge of collapse. If New York were to lose its water supply—much of which is piped from over a hundred miles away—the city could be shut down. Given Manhattan's financial and cultural prominence, this would have global repercussions.

The more I researched water, the more sensitized I became to how we use and abuse it, and what steps we could take to manage water more intelligently. But, like many recent converts, my new-found knowledge sometimes got the best of me, and I became unintentionally preachy. I also discovered that water talk can elicit surprisingly strong emotions in people.

Water is a very personal subject. The human body is 70 percent water, and the health of our water systems has a lot to do with our own health; as animals, we understand this instinctively. Furthermore, water is one of the most durable metaphors in art and literature; it plays a central role in most religions, is a scientifically fascinating subject, and represents many different things to people. Telling people how to use water seems to push a primal red button inside us. At first I found this confusing, but I have come to believe it stems from the fact that water, like air, is a vital resource; any perceived threat to its supply sets off a defensive reaction. Regulating water use is perceived as tantamount to telling people how to live their lives.

One day at the gym I noticed a large guy brushing his teeth very slowly while he allowed the faucet to gush at full blast. I had recently toured the city's Tunnel Number 3 and was acutely aware of how much time, effort, and money went into collecting and transporting that water he was so blithely wasting. As his dental hygiene went on and on, and the precious water drained away, I paced around my locker trying to decide what to do. He eyed me in the mirror and kept up his languorous ablutions. Finally I couldn't take the provocation any longer and said, as politely as possible, "Excuse me, sir, but would you mind turning that water off while you brush? The New York water system—" Before I could get another word out, he spun at me with a red face, shouting curses, and jabbing his foamy toothbrush at my eye. I blinked, stumbled backward, mumbled something, and retreated. Apparently he considered wasting water an inalienable right. I decided to keep my mouth shut in the future.

A year or so later I noticed the same guy doing the same thing in the same place. Again he eyed me in the mirror. This time I said nothing. But to my surprise, he quietly turned off the spigot as he continued brushing.

What's the lesson? Maybe it's not a bad idea to speak up for the right thing, as long as you do so carefully and respectfully.

THE SUMMER OF GLOBAL WEIRDING

Shortly after the publication of *The Ripple Effect,* many of my concerns about water suddenly manifested themselves: record-breaking floods and droughts during the summer of 2011 forced Americans to pay attention to water as never before, whether we wanted to or not.

That August I sat on the stony beach below a family cabin on the coast of Maine, just above the lapping Atlantic. I was wondering how much longer we would be able to enjoy this idyll, for the sea is gobbling up the shoreline and advancing on the house. At the time, Hurricane Irene was just a few hours south of us, and moving up the coast fast; the sky was lowering. We had stocked up on extra candles, batteries, and whiskey, and now all we could do was wait. In the primeval forest behind the cabin, many old fir and spruce trees had been weakened by winter storms and blight, and I feared they'd be knocked down, perhaps onto the house. Earlier that summer Maine had turned unusually dry, and wells had sputtered; but then the rain and fog moved in, and roads and basements flooded. By August the small town nearby had become choked with tourists lured by a national park, the chance to go shopping, and a hunger for lobster, corn, and blueberry pie.

When Irene finally arrived with howling winds and spraying whitecaps, nerves frayed and the single road off the island turned into a virtual parking lot, as people drove into the slashing storm in a frantic attempt to get home. But they should have stayed, for in the end the storm only glanced off our coast. Irene toppled a few trees, knocked out the power, smashed a friend's cabin into kindling, and rearranged some of the massive rocks on the beach. But it blew away after a couple of days, and in the end was relatively anticlimactic.

Then the phone rang: it was my sister, calling from Brattleboro, Vermont. Her town, deep inland, had been hammered by ferocious gusts and nearly washed away in record rains. The road in front of her house, Route 9, the main east–west corridor in that part of the state, had been transformed into a ravine. Some of her neighbors were trapped in their homes. At least forty people died statewide, millions of dollars of damage was done, bridges and buildings vanished, and a state of emergency was declared. Then people began to run out of drinking water. A few days later, the *New York Times* reported that Irene had caused about $10 billion worth of damage and was one of the ten costliest disasters in US history.

As I raked up limbs in Maine, it struck me that this was a vision of the world as my children might know it: one in which the weather will become increasingly violent, unpredictable, and capricious.

Why did Irene batter inland Vermont and merely brush coastal Maine? The only answer I could come up with was: pure luck. Yet it seems that every year there are more deadly hurricanes, tornadoes, tsunamis, sharp temperature shifts, and prolonged floods and droughts than ever, across the country and around the world. Water is a key component to all of these phenomena.

Indeed, 2011 was a remarkable year for water-related weather. Much of the West was saturated by record floods—the Mississippi reached levels higher than the infamous flood of 1927, while Montana had record snowfall and Iowa, Nebraska, and Missouri were flooded through the fall. At the same time, fourteen states across the South were afflicted by withering drought—Texas, Oklahoma, and New Mexico faced their driest conditions in history, even worse than the Dust Bowl of the 1930s—and were scorched by wildfires that consumed thousands of acres. Despite our ability to predict storms more accurately and respond more quickly than ever, these "extreme weather events" resulted in hundreds of deaths and billions of dollars' worth of devastation.

That's just in the United States. Floods and droughts afflicted Europe, Africa, and Asia. Some places have faced both phenomena. In 2011, Australia emerged from a multiyear drought only to be deluged by a flood so severe it has been called "the worst natural disaster in Australian history." Numerous Western European nations—including Britain, France, Germany, and Switzerland—faced unusual heat, followed by flash floods. China faced a once-in-one-hundred-year drought, followed by a record rainfall that killed ninety-four people and displaced thousands. Colombia, Peru, Kenya, Somalia, and Bangladesh have seen record high temperatures, while other small nations, such as Nepal, have experienced record rains.

The international humanitarian consortium Oxfam reports that human disasters caused by storms and floods have increased from

133 per year in the 1980s to 350 a year today. And the insurance firm Swiss Re estimates that losses from natural disasters have risen from $25 billion annually in the 1980s to $130 billion in 2011.

Some believe 2011's remarkable weather was due to natural climate variability caused by a La Niña event (in which the tropical Pacific cools, and southern states typically get below-average precipitation; in El Niño years, the Pacific warms and the South gets more rain). Others say it is because of climate change. Scientists don't have a definitive answer yet, though many have cautioned that storms such as Katrina and Irene are harbingers of worse to come, as the climate warms and causes some regions to become wetter while others grow drier.

Climate change is a shift in weather patterns over an extended period of time; the change can be in the average weather for a region, or in the distribution of extreme weather events. Historically the climate has heated and cooled slowly, due to changes in the earth's orbit, which affects how much sunlight falls on different parts of the globe. But now the shifts are occurring faster.

Some scientists believe that anthropogenic factors—that is, human-produced greenhouse gases, which trap heat in the atmosphere—are speeding up and worsening the natural flux. John Holdren, formerly of Harvard and now a senior White House science adviser, notes that "global warming" implies a gradual shift in temperature, but a more accurate description of the quickening shifts in weather is "global climatic disruption." I prefer the term coined by Hunter Lovins, cofounder of the Rocky Mountain Institute, who characterizes the shift as "Global Weirding."

There are towers of credible, peer-reviewed research demonstrating that the earth's climate is growing hotter. Yet, in this era of politicized science and inflammatory rhetoric, it is becoming increasingly difficult to discuss global climate change. Much of the public remains skeptical or confused about the issue. Conservative politicians such as Texas Governor Rick Perry proclaim that climate change is a "contrived, phony mess," while Tea Party candidates like Michele Bachmann deride the EPA as a "job-killing agency." As the nation prepares for a national election, the debate over environmental policy has raised a wall of incoherent white noise. Speaking at an Aspen Institute media forum in August 2011, Al Gore lamented, "It's no longer acceptable in mixed company—meaning bipartisan company—to use the goddamn word 'climate.'"

Global warming is speeding up the hydrologic cycle—the rate at which water evaporates into the air and falls to the ground as precipitation. The implications of this are enormous. As the climate warms, there will be more rain and less snow; diminished snowpack will lead to changes in runoff patterns and water supplies; increased evaporation will lead to less soil moisture, which results in erosion, an influx of invasive species, and the spread of pathogens. The warming climate is affecting hydrological infrastructure—dams, reservoirs, levees, aqueducts, pipelines, locks, and the like—and is altering the life cycle of plants, particularly trees. With plentiful rain, plants undergo a growth spurt; in dry periods, they wilt. The extra biomass that results from a growth period creates dry tinder, which can lead to forest fires. Higher temperatures allow invasive species to move into new territory, and destroy it—as bark beetles have notoriously done in the mountain West. As old-growth forests die off or spark into wildfires, the carbon they store is released back into the air, which adds to the greenhouse effect.

Robert Hirsch, the US Geological Survey's former chief hydrologist, notes that climate change also affects water quality: higher water temperatures, more frequent storms, and shifts in water flow affect aquatic life, pollution levels, the oxygen content of water, and turbidity. (Although Hirsch agrees the planet is warming, he cautions, "Scientific evidence about the specific ways it is changing our water resources is still very unclear.")

The United Nations warns of a "looming water crisis," perhaps even water wars in coming decades. These pressures, and the recent spate of extreme weather, have forced people to think about how we value water, and manage it, in new ways.

H₂O SOLUTIONS

The traditional response to drought and flood has been to erect giant hydro-infrastructure—dams, pipelines, levees, and the like—to capture, store, and convey water. In the last century, such projects helped to build the nation. Some politicians are now advocating for even bigger plumbing projects, such as "Flipping the Mississippi," a scheme that would pipe surplus Mississippi floodwater to the parched West. But it has been widely acknowledged that large water diversion projects are expensive, inefficient, environmentally destructive, and politically divisive. In short, they are viewed as nineteenth-century solutions for twenty-first-century problems.

In recent years, a cheaper, more environmentally sound, technology-driven ethos has sprung up. Emphasizing conservation and efficiency, the advocates of "soft path" engineering, such as Peter Gleick of the Pacific Institute, say relatively modest initiatives—using low-flush toilets, low-flow showerheads, front-loading washing machines, drip-irrigated farming, and underground water banking, for example—save more water and money than traditional, "hard path" infrastructure does.

When it comes to controlling flood and drought, smaller nations provide useful lessons for the United States. After a flood killed more than 1,800 people in 1953, Holland spent billions of dollars to build a world-class flood control system. Today, over two-thirds of the Dutch population lives twenty feet below sea level, but thanks to giant floodgates and the innovative use of floodplains, dunes, dikes, retention ponds, and floating houses, the Dutch have protected themselves against a once-in-10,000-year storm. By contrast, much of the United States does not have protection against once-in-one-hundred-year storms. The key to Holland's success is public education about the dangers of flooding, water boards that oversee the funding of flood control projects, and a willingness to work with the environment rather than attempting to dominate it.

When it comes to conservation and efficiency, perhaps no nation uses water so parsimoniously as Singapore. With a population of 4.8 million, the city-state is built on a marshy island and freshwater is treated as a precious resource. Demand is curbed by high water taxes, efficient technologies, and relentless public education. Forty percent of Singapore's water supply comes from Malaysia, while a remarkable 30 percent is provided by desalination and recycled wastewater; the rest is drawn from large-scale rainwater collection and other sources. Singapore has reduced its per capita water use from 165 liters a day in 2003 to 155 in 2010.

Although America is much larger and more complex than Holland or Singapore, these water-smart nations provide useful models we can learn from. They have invested in hydro-infrastructure and emphasized public education about water to a much greater degree than America has. But it wasn't always this way.

A century ago, the United States built a state-of-the-art water system that proved so effective that, ironically, we now take our supply for granted. Our water purification and sewage treatment systems eliminated diseases such as cholera and dysentery that once caused dreadful epidemics. The construction of massive hydro-infrastructure—dams, reservoirs, levees, pipelines, canals and locks, and the like—allowed the "desert to bloom," generated hydroelectricity, powered the nation during the Second World War, and protected communities from drought and flood.

But much of our water infrastructure is collapsing from neglect and age, is insufficient for a growing population, and is insufficient for the storms predicted for the future. In its 2009 Report Card for

America's Infrastructure, the American Society of Civil Engineers gave most US hydro-infrastructure a grade of D-minus. This means it is on the verge of failure. (To take just one example, the EPA estimates that 1 trillion gallons of water leak from domestic pipes every year.) It will take trillions of dollars to dig up and repair pipes, replace old levees and dams, and upgrade canals and locks, and this work will be extraordinarily expensive and inconvenient. Politicians avoid talking about this impending "replacement age" as if it were a dark curse, but we will have to address it. Yes, infrastructure improvement projects are costly, but they will create jobs, save water, improve health, and make the nation safer and more competitive.

About forty years ago, as the direct result of water catastrophes such as the burning of the Cuyahoga River and the disease, miscarriages, and birth defects from toxic waste buried at Love Canal, a bipartisan group of congressional representatives pushed the White House to protect waterways and keep drinking supplies clean by passing the Clean Water Act and the Safe Drinking Water Act, and founding the Environmental Protection Agency. Now the EPA is under attack, many of those regulations are woefully out of date, and meddling by Congress and confusing rulings by the US Supreme Court have made environmental regulation difficult. EPA officials lack clear jurisdiction to prosecute environmental crimes: according to the *New York Times,* 1,500 major pollution cases have not been prosecuted recently because of confusion over jurisdiction. "When companies figure out the cops can't operate, they start remembering how much cheaper it is to just dump stuff in a nearby creek," an EPA lawyer told the newspaper. Our national water laws need updating, and regulators must be empowered to fully enforce them.

We also must do a far better job of educating ourselves about flood mitigation and water conservation, use new technologies— real-time water metering, laser and satellite measurements, desalination, and sewage recycling—and institute meaningful water management policies. Unlike water-smart nations, America does not have a single federal water authority or even a unified set of water laws (in the United States, eastern and western water laws are completely different). It is time to consider creating a new federal water office—appoint a "water czar," say, or a national water board—to manage the nation's supplies holistically and comprehensively.

Perhaps the best way to bring about change is to appeal to people's self-interest. This means we should price water more carefully and use a combination of financial incentives and penalties to nudge people into conserving water and preserving its cleanliness. This isn't simply a matter of "doing the right thing." As *New York Times* columnist and best-selling author Thomas Friedman argues, nations that use resources more efficiently in the twenty-first century will outperform those that are inefficient.

Reinventing how we think about water, and manage it, will be difficult and expensive. But as I sat on our receding beach in Maine, contemplating the depredations of Hurricane Irene, the dying forest, and the hungry crowds of people in the background, I realized that in the Age of Global Weirding we don't have a choice.

RIPPLE EFFECTS

I called my book *The Ripple Effect* because every time we use freshwater, even for something as basic as washing our hands, spraying the lawn, or generating electricity, it sets off a ripple effect—a series of hydrologic consequences, which most people are unaware of.

When you wash your hands with antibacterial soap, for example, you flush the chemical triclocarban into waterways, where it leaves fish vulnerable to disease. If you spray your lawn or crops with the weed killer atrazine, the chemicals, suspected carcinogens, may cause male fish to produce eggs in their testes. Why is this important?

Well, the human endocrine system is very similar to a fish's, and scientists are concerned that in our zeal to eradicate dandelions we may be doing grievous harm to ourselves without realizing it.

Another kind of ripple is set off when you power up your computer or leave the lights on. Electricity is generated by hydroelectric dams, or by coal, gas, nuclear, or ethanol-fueled plants, all of which use huge amounts of water. The water taken by industry, and the pollution emitted into waterways, profoundly affects the ecosystem, and us. And so it goes, on and on, as the ripples of our actions emanate outward, often without our understanding.

But now, in the second decade of the twenty-first century, we no longer have the luxury of ignorance. We have a better understanding of our personal and societal ripple effect than ever before: We know how we impact water supplies, what we can do to mitigate that impact, and where to look for solutions to our water questions. What's lacking is the will to do something about it.

Humans tend to wait for a crisis before taking action. But with water, if we wait for a crisis, it will be too late. We know this, for water *is* life. To avoid a water crisis, we must adapt to the new hydrologic reality. Or, as Albert Einstein put it, "Those who have the privilege to know have the duty to act."

So let's take action. Let's learn to value water more highly and use it more sustainably, and then let's send those *positive* ripples out into the world. There is no time to waste.

Part II | WHERE DO WE GO FROM HERE?

6

A WAY FORWARD?

The Soft Path for Water

Peter H. Gleick

Peter H. Gleick is an internationally recognized water expert whose work addresses the critical connections between water and health, the human right to water, the hydrologic impacts of climate change, sustainable water use, privatization and globalization, and ways of reducing conflicts over water resources.

Gleick received a bachelor's degree from Yale University in engineering and applied science, and master's and doctoral degrees from the Energy and Resources Group of the University of California at Berkeley. He has received numerous awards for his work, among them the prestigious MacArthur "Genius" Fellowship in 2003 for exemplary contributions to water resources. He was elected to the US National Academy of Sciences in 2006, named "a visionary on the environment" by the BBC, and identified as "one of 15 people the next president should listen to" by *Wired* magazine. Gleick serves on the boards of numerous organizations and journals, is the author of more than one hundred peer-reviewed scientific papers and book chapters, and has authored or edited nine books, including the acclaimed series *The World's Water: The Biennial Report on Freshwater Resources* and *Bottled and Sold: The Story Behind Our Obsession with Bottled Water*.

Things are changing in the world of water. The United States uses less water today than it used thirty years ago, for everything, despite an exponentially growing population and economy. The United Nations has declared a formal human right to water. Countries are rewriting their national constitutions and laws to guarantee water for natural ecosystems and the poor. Farmers are constantly learning how to grow more food with less water and fewer water-contaminating chemicals.

In the poorest regions of the world, new efforts are being made to provide basic water and sanitation services, to let young girls who now have to spend hours collecting water attend school instead, and to ensure that water is being used for productive economic purposes. In the richer nations, new technologies are permitting industries to produce more goods and services with less water, and to clean used water to higher and higher standards, while leaving more water in rivers and streams for natural ecosystems.

And the changes are reaching down to the personal level. At my house, we've replaced old toilets, showerheads, and faucets with ones that use a fraction of the water and do a better job. Our washing machine uses only 65 percent of the water our old one used, and it does a better job cleaning our clothes while also using less energy. We removed the grass in our backyard and put in far more attractive water-efficient landscaping. We eat less water-intensive meat. We don't buy bottled water but drink our excellent tap water, unfiltered. We now use half the water of the average Californian, our total water use continues to drop, and our lifestyle hasn't suffered as a consequence.

So the good news is that although there is no shortage of global freshwater problems, there is also no shortage of innovative solutions to those problems, if we can only find the commitment and will to implement them more consistently, broadly, and rapidly.

But there is plenty of bad water news as well. The amount of water on the planet has remained unchanged for billions of years, while the world's population, now more than 7 billion, is using more and more of the world's limited freshwater each year. We have to meet expanding human and environmental needs under increasingly difficult conditions and with increasingly stressed resources. And despite great advances in recent years, we're still doing an inadequate job of managing our water resources for either the current or future generations.

Too many people still lack safe water or adequate sanitation services.[1] Too many children die every year from preventable water-related diseases. Too many natural ecosystems are being destroyed by human withdrawals of water. Extensive industrial activities have created massive water demand and produced contaminants that nature has no way of recycling or absorbing and that end up in our soil, air, and water. The global climate is changing because of industrialization, which among other things is leading to changes in water availability and quality and to a growing risk of floods and droughts.

It is time for a new approach and a new way of thinking about water development, use, and management—what I call the "soft path for water."

The concept of the soft path has been developing and evolving for several decades as we have come to realize that old ways of addressing water and other resource challenges are no longer adequate. This chapter provides an overview of those old approaches, why they have failed in the twenty-first century, and how the soft path might offer a way forward out of our current water problems. And the best news is that many soft path ideas and practices are already being implemented, slowly moving the world in the right direction.

---

1 World Health Organization and UN Children's Fund Joint Monitoring, Programme for Water Supply and Sanitation, "Progress on Drinking Water and Sanitation: Special Focus on Sanitation," UNICEF, New York, and WHO, Geneva, Switzerland, 2008.

THE THREE AGES OF WATER

Humanity's interactions and experiences with water have evolved over the past several thousand years. Looking back through the lens of history, we can see the transitions from one water age to another and the forces that drove those changes.

The First Age of Water began when Homo sapiens emerged as thinking, communal beings. In this era, the water we needed was simply taken from the environment with little thought, planning, or management. The natural hydrologic cycle of evaporation, condensation, precipitation, evaporation, and runoff purified water and delivered it to us in rivers, streams, lakes, and natural springs fed by rain and snowmelt. Hunter/gatherer societies had little knowledge of agriculture or need for irrigation or flood control, and their interactions with water were simple and limited.

The Second Age of Water began when humans began to develop more formal fixed communities and to realize the advantages of intentionally modifying and managing the water around them. The development of agriculture led to the invention of artificial irrigation. The populations of these early communities grew, soon outstripping their local water resources and leading people to begin intentionally moving and storing water from the landscapes around them. In this age, we see the first irrigation canals, aqueducts, acequias (gravity-powered water conduits), artificial dams for storage and flood control, and groundwater wells to tap aquifers. And we see these modifications everywhere in the archaeological record. It is no accident that the greatest early civilizations arose on the banks of perennial rivers, such as the Tigris, Euphrates, Indus, Ganges, Nile, and Jordan. Wherever traces of ancient civilizations are found, we also find traces of early hydraulic engineers moving, storing, and treating water. And some of these ancient water supply systems are still in operation—for example, the Acequia Real in Granada, Spain, built in the 1230s, which still delivers water to the Alhambra.

These early hydrological engineering developments were also accompanied by advances in the institutions and laws for managing water. The Code of Hammurabi, a legal code written in the eighteenth century BCE by an early king of ancient Babylon, includes rules for managing the region's precious water resources, including the rational and fair distribution of irrigation water, how to maintain physical water systems, and punishments for water theft. The cities of ancient Greece were often planned around water sources and municipal institutions were created to manage them. Roman cities were built with water systems of remarkable sophistication and precision.

The Second Water Age culminated in the nineteenth and twentieth centuries, when the planet's population finally outgrew nature's ability to provide adequate water at adequate quality for our needs. In response, the technological innovators behind the Industrial Revolution turned their attention to developing sophisticated and centralized chemical, mechanical, biological, and institutional systems that mimic and magnify nature's hydrologic cycle. Modern water treatment systems that flocculate, coagulate, precipitate, condense, and distill water are simply mechanical imitations of natural processes. Where nature uses the sun, gravity, and biological systems, humans developed artificial pumping, chemistry, and mechanical means to mimic nature. Massive sand or charcoal filters copy and magnify the purification role played by soil. We run water through reverse osmosis membranes that imitate the ability of living cells to separate salts from solution. We purify water with high-intensity ultraviolet lamps or ozonation, which replicate the effects of the sun and atmospheric chemistry. We use naturally occurring waste-eating bacteria that take the biological products in wastewater and consume them, producing fertilizer, oxygen, and energy. We distill water in massive boilers and condensers powered by fossil fuels that are concentrated mechanical reproductions of the hydrologic cycle. We rely on dams to capture and store water when it rains so that we can use it when it doesn't; long aqueducts to move water from wet regions to dry regions; complex sets of pumps and artificial irrigation equipment to produce our food; hydroelectric power stations to create the energy needed to produce goods and services; and treatment plants, distribution pipelines, wastewater collection systems, and waste treatment plants to satisfy the needs of cities and industries that have long outgrown their local water resources.

These transformations in how society manages water have been unheralded, gradual, and mostly unnoticed by society, overshadowed by more visible technological developments such as aviation, the automobile, and the computer—but modern civilization could not have developed without them.

We are now in the midst of another transition, to the Third Age of Water. The Second Age brought enormous benefits, but it ultimately failed to satisfy the universal human needs for water and water services, while also failing to protect the natural ecosystems on which we all depend. We know that we must change direction if we are going to ultimately solve our global water problems and move to a truly sustainable planet. This requires a new approach that meets basic human needs for water for all while living within the constraints of a limited resource, protecting natural ecosystems, and addressing the growing challenges of climate change.

There are two primary ways of meeting water-related needs. One path—the "hard path"—relies almost exclusively on the advances, ideas, and institutions of the Second Age of Water, especially centralized infrastructure and decision-making: dams and reservoirs, pipelines and treatment plants, water departments and agencies. It delivers water, mostly of potable quality, and takes away wastewater.

Work on defining and implementing an alternative "soft path" for water has been under way, quietly and slowly, since the mid-1990s.[2] The soft path focuses on delivering water "services," not just

2   P. H. Gleick, P. Loh, S. V. Gomez, and J. Morrison, "California Water 2020: A Sustainable Vision," Pacific Institute for Studies in Development, Environment, and Security, Oakland, California, 1995.

water, and doing so in a way that supports both human and ecosystem needs. Like the hard path, it relies on centralized infrastructure but complements it with extensive investment in decentralized facilities, efficient technologies, and human capital.[3] The soft path strives to improve the overall productivity of water use rather than to seek endless sources of new supply. It delivers water services carefully matched to needs, satisfies different water needs with waters of appropriate quality, and is far more inclusive of water users at local and community scales. In short, it is the right path to the Third Age of Water.

SOFT VERSUS HARD: SIX KEY DIFFERENCES

The approaches developed and applied in the Second Era of Water, successful as they were, are increasingly recognized as inadequate for the water challenges that now face us. We must find new answers, but the process of defining, developing, and implementing an alternative path has not yet been completed. Moreover, traditional and powerful political, social, and economic entities in the water sector continue to pursue old approaches because they do not understand the new options available to us, they do not believe they will be effective, or they have vested interests to defend. Our universities still teach old approaches to water management with a focus on engineering and infrastructure supported by consulting and construction companies. Water managers and policy makers continue to focus on traditional solutions, believing that we must do more of what we've always done and that the hard path is still the best way to meet global water needs.

---

3 P. H. Gleick, "Soft Water Paths," *Nature,* July 25, 2002, 373.

Part of the challenge is that the planet as a whole is in a difficult transition. The serious environmental threats posed by our burgeoning global population and current styles of industrial and agricultural development are real and are not going to be solved by traditional thinking and approaches. But although it is increasingly apparent that our current path is unsustainable, there is no clear agreement on a new path forward. An active and often contentious discussion is still under way about the definitions, strategies, and implementation of "sustainable development." But we all can agree that too many rivers are running dry, droughts and floods are devastating too many local communities, water contamination from human and industrial waste is out of control, millions still die from unnecessary and preventable water-related diseases, and there is growing violence over water access and control. We cannot continue with business as usual.

The soft path includes the growing understanding that there are important *nonstructural* components of a comprehensive approach to sustainable water management and use that must complement the hard components we traditionally build. In the work that I and my colleagues have done, the soft and hard paths differ in at least six ways:[4]

1. The soft path provides water-related goods and services, not just water itself, efficiently and comprehensively. For example, people want to be able to cook, clean themselves and their belongings, grow food, and produce goods and services. They usually don't have an ideological preference for how much water is used in the pursuit of these activities, and indeed may not care whether any water is used at all. Water agencies

---

4 G. Wolff and P. H. Gleick, "Soft Water Paths," in P. H. Gleick, *The World's Water 2002–2003* (Washington, DC: Island Press, 2002), 1–32.

must rethink how to provide *water services* more effectively rather than simply providing *water*.

2. Water comes in many different qualities. So do water demands. But we rarely try to match the quality of supply with the quality of demands. The soft path recognizes the advantages of reserving higher-quality water for those uses that *require* higher quality—for example, drinking water or certain high-value industrial processes that require pure water, such as semiconductor or pharmaceutical production. At the same time, lower-quality waters, such as storm water, gray water, and some forms of recycled water, can satisfy demands that do not require potable water, such as outdoor landscaping, industrial cooling, or flushing toilets. The tradition of providing potable water to all users regardless of need inflates the true amounts of water actually needed and the costs of providing it.

3. The soft path recognizes that investments in small-scale and decentralized alternatives can often provide benefits that are comparable to or even better than investments in traditional large-scale, centralized options. The soft path also recognizes the "co-benefits" available from new approaches, where improvements in water reliability, quality, energy use, environmental conditions, and equity may all come together.

4. The soft path recognizes that ecological health and the human activities that depend on it (such as recreational activities, fishing, tourism, and delivery of clean raw water to downstream users) are core benefits often unrecognized (and unmonetized) by traditional hard path approaches. The hard path assumes that all water should be used for an economically productive purpose rather than being left in a river, stream, or lake, while failing to recognize or account for losses in ecological value of this strategy, causing serious ecological destruction throughout the world.

5. The soft path offers new thinking about water economics, including the power of "economies of scope." Although the
   hard path looks at projects, revenues, and economies of scale,
   economies of scope exist when a combined decision-making
   process allows combinations of specific services to be delivered
   at lower cost than would result from separate decision-making
   processes. Thus, sustainable water policy now recognizes the
   benefits to water agencies and providers when they work together with land-use planners, flood protection agencies, and
   energy utilities.

6. Finally, the soft path encourages far more public participation
   and community decision-making than the hard path, which
   relies on traditional engineering approaches, consulting/
   construction firms, and centralized government agencies and
   funding strategies. Effective engagement with water users is
   necessary to avoid the adverse impacts of traditional water
   development and also to more clearly understand what communities need and want in the way of water services.

A FOCUS ON IMPROVING WATER PRODUCTIVITY AND EFFICIENCY RATHER THAN WATER SUPPLY

There are many dimensions to the soft path for water, and improvements are needed in a comprehensive set of technologies, policies,
and institutions.[5] But in all discussions of this approach, a key ele-
ment is improving the efficiency and productivity of water use.

Improving efficiency is not a new concept, but until now it has
not played a central role in water planning. More than six decades

---

5 P. H. Gleick, "The Changing Water Paradigm: A Look at Twenty-First-Century Water
Resources Development," *Water International* 25, no. 1 (2000): 127–138.

ago, the Water Resources Policy Commission of the United States published *A Water Policy for the American People,* which observed:

> We can no longer be wasteful and careless in our attitude towards our water resources. Not only in the West, where the crucial value of water has long been recognized, but in every part of the country, we must manage and conserve water if we are to make the best use of it for future development.[6]

In the early 1960s Gilbert White, a pioneer of innovative water thinking, called for broadening the range of alternatives examined by water managers who had previously focused only on structural solutions to water problems. In an early hint of the developing soft path approach, White called on resource managers to consider non-structural alternatives to traditional infrastructure, including the use of zoning, land-use planning, and changing water-use patterns.[7]

The soft path also focuses on nonstructural approaches to improving water-use efficiency and productivity—the reduction in water use while maintaining or even improving social benefits. In this approach, the goal is to minimize the use of water while maximizing the benefits that water provides. There are many ways to measure water-use efficiency or productivity, such as the amount of measurable output per unit of water that is used. The units of output can be physical (for example, tons of wheat or rice, numbers of cars) or economic (such as the dollar value of the good or service produced).

---

6 Water Resources Policy Commission, *A Water Policy for the American People, The Report of the President's Water Resources Policy Commission, Volume 1* (Washington, DC: US Government Printing Office, 1950).

7 G. F. White, "The Choices of Use in Resource Management," *Natural Resources Journal* 1 (1961): 23–40.

Figure 6.1 shows water productivity for the US economy from 1950 through 2005, measured in dollars of gross national product (GNP) per unit of water used. When water was considered abundant in the mid-twentieth century, water-use productivity was relatively constant. In the 1970s, a combination of factors began to cause water productivity to improve. These factors included rising environmental awareness, new regulations restricting uncontrolled dumping of wastewater, improvements in water-using technologies, and the shift in the structure of the US economy toward the service sector and away from water-intensive industries. Water productivity has now increased substantially and is more than double its value in the 1970s, even correcting for the effects of inflation.

The increase in water productivity is especially critical in the agricultural sector. Agriculture is the largest user of water worldwide, consuming around 80 percent of the water that humans mobilize. And improving productivity of water use in agriculture means

Fig. 6.1. U.S. economic productivity of water from 1950 to 2005 in dollars of GNP per hundred gallons of water used.

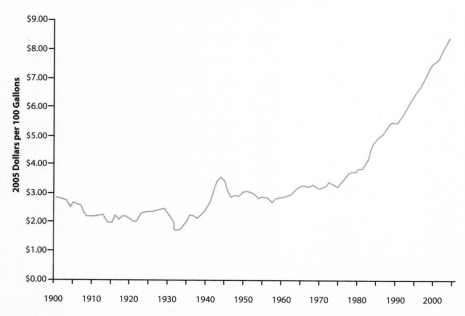

it is possible to grow more food and fiber with less water on less land, which is critical for meeting the food needs of the world's billions of people.

There are many ways to increase agricultural water-use efficiency, including land leveling to reduce wasteful runoff, new methods of seeding that take advantage of soil moisture, drip irrigation and precision sprinklers to deliver water to the right place at the right time, better soil-moisture monitoring to improve the timing of irrigation deliveries, and lining of aqueducts to prevent seepage. A recent study on California agriculture shows that a range of soft-path approaches to improving the efficiency of water use can save 15 percent or more of current water use while maintaining or even increasing crop production and farmer income.[8] Similar results have been found around the world.

These kinds of approaches, individually and in combination, can help satisfy the world's growing water constraints, reduce unsustainable overpumping of groundwater, and help leave water in natural systems to restore the health of ecosystems—all soft-path objectives. Moreover, these strategies are almost always cheaper and faster to implement than traditional alternatives currently being proposed. For example, matching the potential agricultural water savings in California would require building between three and twenty new dams—and there are no longer enough places in the state to build dams that are economically, environmentally, or politically acceptable.

Substantial amounts of water are also used to produce goods and services in the residential, commercial, industrial, and institutional sectors. As with agriculture, a wide range of approaches can be used to improve water-use efficiency in urban settings, including

8 H. Cooley, J. Christian-Smith, and P. H. Gleick, "More with Less: The Potential for Agricultural Water Conservation and Efficiency in California," Pacific Institute, Oakland, California, September 2008.

new technologies, pricing policies, educational strategies, voluntary and mandatory regulations, and more. A number of municipal water suppliers have implemented aggressive water conservation programs, especially (but not exclusively) in water-short arid and semi-arid regions throughout the world. Wherever such efforts have been made, reductions on the order of 10 percent to 30 percent in urban use have been readily obtained. Recently California passed legislation asking for an additional 20 percent reduction in per capita urban water use by 2020. Despite the fact that many urban agencies in the state have been implementing a wide range of conservation programs for many decades, a recent study by the Pacific Institute concluded that urban savings potential in California is still on the order of 30 percent or more of total water use. Examples of both indoor and outdoor savings were identified in every sector, for every end use.[9]

Many water managers and planners still believe that using less water somehow means a loss of prosperity or a constraint on development. The traditional assumption is that continued growth in population and improvements in economic well-being require continued increases in water withdrawals and consumption. This is no longer true: the link between water use and economic well-being is not immutable. It can be weakened, modified, and even broken, as it already has been in the United States. This can be seen in Figure 6.2, which shows water withdrawals (in cubic kilometers per year, with each cubic kilometer equal to around 264 billion gallons) and gross domestic product (in year 2000 dollars) for the United States from 1900 to 2005. Up until 1980 these curves rose together, and increases in national income were matched by similar increases in

---

9 P. H. Gleick, D. Haasz, C. Henges-Jeck, V. Srinivasan, G. Wolff, K. Kao Cushing, and A. Mann, "Waste Not, Want Not: The Potential for Urban Water Conservation in California," Pacific Institute, Oakland, California, November 2003.

Fig. 6.2. U.S. GNP and water withdrawals 1900 to 2005. Note how the curves went up together until the late 1970s and early 1980s, when total U.S. water withdrawals leveled and even declined.

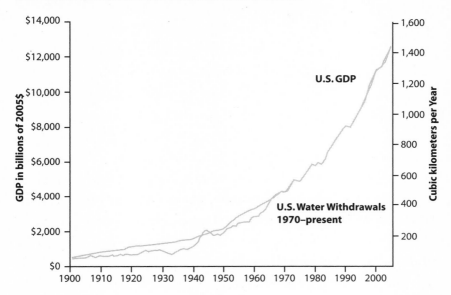

water withdrawals. After the late 1970s and early 1980s this relationship changed, with continued rapid increases in national income but a leveling off and even a decline in total water withdrawals. Similar patterns can be seen in other parts of the world as well.

MOVING FORWARD ON THE SOFT PATH

The transition from the Second to the Third Age of Water will take time. Although the failures of the Second Age to solve all of our water challenges are readily apparent, the water crisis means different things in different places, and the urgency and ability to address it varies greatly. Ultimately, however, there is no avoiding the challenges of unconstrained population growth, growing ecological damages from excessive or inappropriate water use, and the failure to meet basic water needs for billions of people. Things will have to change.

Fortunately, there are viable ways of moving forward on the soft path for water. The first step is realizing that traditional approaches are inadequate and that new ways of thinking are needed, including especially the need to move from a focus on new sources of supply to one on increasing water-use efficiency and productivity.

The second step is to identify the existing barriers to changing the way we deal with water and to develop tools for overcoming those barriers. The third step is to make social choices about the importance of new water policies in a world with conflicting problems and priorities. Finally, government agencies, local communities, water agencies, and the private sector must make serious commitments to solve our water problems once and for all.

As we move into the Third Age of Water, sustainable water management and use will require complex combinations of approaches, including flexible regulation, economic incentives and markets, improvements in water purification technologies, and public education and commitment. Recent experiences in every sector of the economy suggest that the most effective water programs include combinations of these approaches rather than narrow, single-answer solutions.

Flexible regulations include policies taken by governments to encourage standards for the efficiency of new technologies, improved water-quality regulations and monitoring, the adoption of landscape ordinances, and new efficient building codes and designs. Economic incentives and markets include new water rate structures that include strategies such as marginal cost volumetric water prices, rebates from energy or water utilities for more efficient appliances or practices, low-cost loans or grants to help finance technological improvements, and environmental fees that allow the true costs of resource use or degradation to be recovered. The creation of local water markets to permit users to move water to different uses can also increase the efficient allocation and use of water, assuming such markets also protect environmental values.

New technologies permit the cleaning and reuse of any quality of water, accurate monitoring of water quality and uses, advanced media and informational techniques to communicate with water users and managers, and increasingly affordable desalination. Finally, educational opportunities abound for providing information to the public and policy makers about alternatives to failed water policies. Smart water choices will be demanded and made only when those choices are known and understood.

THE CHOICE WE FACE

The world is in the midst of a transition to a new way of thinking about the world's freshwater resources and the challenges of a world in which billions of people still lack basic water services and millions die from preventable water-related diseases. In the new Third Age of Water, we must move toward sustainable management and use of our vital and limited freshwater resources. New sources of supply, such as recycled water, rainwater harvesting, conjunctive groundwater use, and some forms of desalination, will have to supplement traditional ones. The efficiency of water use will have to improve so we can feed more people with less water and provide more goods and services without taking more water from natural systems. Our damaged aquatic ecosystems will have to be restored and protected.

It's time to make a choice about which water path to take. The traditional hard path for addressing our water problem is well traveled and familiar, but we also are increasingly aware that this path may not lead to the future we want. Instead, it leads to increasing environmental impoverishment, unmet human needs, centralized decision-making, and higher economic and social costs. The other path—a soft path—is also uncertain, but experience suggests it is far more likely to lead us to a desirable future with more productive use of water, more equitable distribution and use of water, improvements in ecological and environmental values, and open, democratic, and transparent institutions.

History suggests that most institutional changes take place slowly, after concerted social action or after crises force action. We must choose our water path and our water future carefully. In the end, the transition to a sustainable planet will also require a transition to a soft path for water.

7

IN OUR LIFETIME

Deconstructing the Global
Water Crisis and Securing Safe Water for All

Gary White

Gary White is CEO and cofounder of Water.org. His vision is simple: to ensure that everyone in the world is able to take a safe drink of water in our lifetime. White's belief that this goal is attainable is rooted in more than two decades in the water sector, learning to discern what works and what does not. His entrepreneurial vision has driven innovations in the way water and sanitation projects are delivered and financed, and these innovations now serve as a model in the sector.

White is a founding board member of the Millennium Water Alliance and Water Advocates, a fellow of the British American Project, a member of the Philanthropy World Hall of Fame, adviser to the Clinton Global Initiative, and a Skoll Social Entrepreneur. Additionally, White was named to the 2011 *Time* 100, the magazine's annual list of the "100 most influential people in the world." Water.org's New Ventures Fund will allow the organization to discover, pilot, and scale the next game-changing solutions in water and sanitation.

We envision the day when everyone in the world can take a safe drink of water. It will be in our lifetime, and this is how we can do it.

WE ARE MORE ALIKE
THAN WE ARE DIFFERENT

Here in the United States and in other countries of the developed world, we are lucky.

The taps in our homes open easily to offer clean water to quench a dry throat or make a cup of tea, to wash dishes or clothing, to water a lawn, or to drench a sweaty child on a hot summer day. We greet each day clean and refreshed. For most people living in the United States today, stories of older relatives who pumped water or trudged to an outhouse are dusted off for family gatherings like well-loved artifacts. See how far we've come? Here, at the top of the consumer pyramid, our lives are easy in ways that have become utterly invisible to us, the heroic solutions to our water problems of yester-century neither remembered nor celebrated.

The contrast, for the nearly 1 billion people who don't have affordable access to clean water, is stark. They walk miles, wait for hours, and pay extortive prices for this fundamental need. There is no rest: every day someone, usually a woman or a girl, has to secure water for her family. There is no way to predict from day to day how long it will take, how much it will cost, how clean the water will be, or how dangerous the journey will be. She may have to fight with other people. She may have to use a dirty cloth to filter out the manure from the cow she elbowed out of the way to fill the jug. The money she set aside for school, books, and shoes goes instead to a loan shark who provided the cash she needed to buy water from the local vendor when the price spiked. But she may wonder how the next slum over got a public water tap, or why the well that was promised by the government agency or nongovernmental organization (NGO) she'd never heard of didn't arrive.

This stark reality has inspired noble and necessary philanthropic efforts to help stop the suffering. There are conferences, master plans, frameworks, legislation, new institutions, and even firmer resolutions. Money is raised. Wells are dug, ribbons are cut. But even after decades of charity, subsidies, multilateral aid, and investments on the part of developing country governments and outside NGOs, the system remains inefficient and largely misses the goal of providing relief for those at the base of the economic pyramid (BOP) in their daily need to secure water. The intentions are good, but the relief is not trickling down. And the "system" that has calcified around the water crisis relies on outdated tools and thinking that is often more likely to keep people in poverty than to lift them out. To the outside observer, it can all seem insane.

Traditional donors tend to scour the top line for signs their investment was fruitful. Although helpful, pursuing metrics based on people reached or project sustainability does not reflect progress toward changing the fundamental constraints of the charity-driven approach, which sees 1 billion potential "beneficiaries." People and communities served by even the most well-intentioned charity program don't feel any sense of ownership of a project that is provided to them. Without that sense of ownership, they will lack the incentive to maintain and repair a well drilled by an outside agency, even if the required parts and skills are locally available. And yet a well maintained solely by outside charity for generations is a poor use of philanthropic resources, sure to leave other people and communities without—because there simply is not enough charity in the world to continue operating like this.

Furthermore, it is a misperception that people and communities in developing countries are uniformly too poor to pay for services such as water. Without a doubt, there are troubling numbers of humans at the absolute base of the economic pyramid who cannot afford to meet even their own most basic needs. These people need and deserve subsidies—but the category of "poor" is no more monolithic than the categories of "middle class" or "wealthy." Poor people without access to water systems (especially in urban and peri-urban areas) often pay informal providers 7 to 15 times more per liter for water than their middle-class or wealthy counterparts. For example, in Port-au-Prince, Haiti, people living in slums get safe water by purchasing eight-ounce plastic sachets of purified water at a per-ounce cost 250 times greater than New York City tap water. The price inequities are unjust, but reveal an opportunity for positive change.

Instead of charity beneficiaries, we must think about the 1 billion people who are living and dying for water access as customers with financial power, rights, responsibilities, and energy to design their own futures. We must measure success by (1) how many poor people are able to pay a fair price for a connection to an existing, modern water system; (2) their satisfaction with that service; and (3) their ability to hold legitimate vendors and local governments accountable for service quality. Through the simple dignity of becoming a paying water customer, the poor are transformed from charity recipients into an economic and political force to be reckoned with. Microfinance-inspired models are helping make this happen.

Financing Debt for Social Change: One Family's Story

Muniyamma lives in an Indian slum with her husband, daughter, son-in-law, and grandson. A public tap was the only source of drinking water for her and the twenty other families on her street. There were often lines and fights at the unreliable water source, which might flow as early as three A.M. or be dry for days.

Because the public tap couldn't meet all of their water needs, other family members took turns collecting contaminated water from agricultural farmland more than a mile away. When Muniyamma learned about WaterCredit and how she could take out a small loan at a low interest rate to get clean water for her household, she took action. In fact, she was the first person in her village to take out a WaterCredit loan and install a reliable source of clean water at her home, paving the way for others to follow.

Sensing an opportunity for powerful synergy with existing microfinance institutions (MFIs), Water.org pioneered WaterCredit, a model in which MFIs expand their services to include loans targeted to meet clients' water and sanitation needs (ranging from rainharvesting tanks to initial utility connections). Microfinance is the provision of financial products and services to economically active poor people who would not otherwise have such access. Microfinance includes both microcredit (the provision of small loans) and, where possible, savings and deposit mobilization.

The concept of microfinance has been around for centuries, but what's commonly called modern microfinance got started in the 1970s with the creation of Grameen Bank by Muhammad Yunus in Bangladesh. Since that time, microfinance has expanded dramatically and is now a global phenomenon, serving over 100 million poor people in countries around the world. It has also become increasingly commercialized, and in many developing countries is now a pillar of the financial sector, representing and serving the needs and interests of those living at the base of the economic pyramid.

Microcredit revolutionized access to capital by making small loans available to poor people for entrepreneurial ventures. Instead of traditional economic collateral, microfinance relies on social collateral—accountability within communities or networks—to ensure loan repayment. WaterCredit uses proven microfinance approaches to develop a proxy for precise market segmentation—to identify and serve the many people like Muniyamma (see sidebar) who can and will pay for water. These approaches also provide a conceptual structure for debt financing for household water and sanitation solutions.

Through WaterCredit, Water.org uses donor funds to leverage commercial capital to fund MFI loan portfolios—substituting a market approach for straight charity. Donor funds are leveraged by helping to underwrite start-up and related software activities of MFIs that are developing water and sanitation portfolios for the first time.

In certain cases, Water.org may provide credit enhancements, such as guarantees and standby letters of credit, to MFIs to assist in portfolio growth. Water.org also provides a variety of capacity-building grants, or "smart subsidies," to its MFI partners for specific purposes, such as water and sanitation market assessments and loan product development, structuring, and rollout.

MFIs participating in WaterCredit typically accrue capital by taking out loans from commercial banks. With that capital, MFIs provide microloans to borrowers seeking to improve access to potable water or sanitation for their families or communities. The global average cost of a WaterCredit loan is around $130, and the majority of loans are disbursed through women's self-help groups or joint-liability groups. Globally, 97 percent of WaterCredit loans are repaid.

To be successful, any microloan must be market-driven in terms of products and terms offered. Water.org supports access to a wide range of water and sanitation products, including household water and sewer connections, rain-harvesting tanks, ventilated pit latrines, and flush toilets. WaterCredit interest rates are determined by what is socially acceptable while also covering the MFI's capital and operating costs. (Some countries also regulate microcredit interest rates.)

As people repay their microloans over time, this effectively "recycles" that capital by leveraging still more loans with that same initial investment. Taking into consideration repayment and redisbursement rates, this microfinance approach can reach five to ten times as many people as a traditional grant over a ten-year period. More organizations are taking up this approach in Africa and Asia. Water.org's efforts alone with this approach are on track to reach 1 million people by 2014 and have the potential to scale even faster as more groups emulate the model. The WaterCredit.org learning platform enables them to do just that.

Millions of current and potential microfinance clients desire a household connection to the water grid, yet utilities have not typically recognized this untapped market. In response to this disconnect, Water.org is conducting market research and piloting initiatives to demonstrate to utilities that people in poor urban and peri-urban communities are able and willing to pay for water services. Companies or investors are unlikely to devote resources to a new product unless they are confident in the return on their investment. Yet an assurance of minimum sales or financial returns for a period of time—an advanced market commitment—can jump-start markets. This approach has been used to spur development of vaccines for pneumococcal disease, and Water.org intends to use it to effectively guarantee a customer base for utilities and reduce the risk for private investors.

AND NOW IT'S TIME TO DO MORE

To get a line of sight on our vision of safe water for all, we must fundamentally change the system. There will always be a need for pure charity to serve the ultrapoor who require subsidies. But for millions more, the introduction of simple, well-designed products and services that speak to their specific needs can make all the difference in their world and ours.

To change the system, we must identify and tap forces that appear unrelated or irrelevant to help solve a problem in an unexpected way. I call this "orthogonal" thinking. Orthogonal thinking serves as an inspirational touchstone to help lead us away from the traditional philanthropic model that has emphasized donor satisfaction over recipient needs, and inject fresh thinking into a sector that has been slow to take advantage of new technologies, financial innovations, and cultural changes. We must open ourselves to, and fund, innovations—creating things like mobile apps, financing mechanisms, citizen engagement tools, and things we haven't thought of yet. Some people and organizations are beginning to experiment in these areas, but we need this to become the norm, not the exception. This process will be iterative, and we should expect to create next-generation products based on what we've learned from their prototypes. We should expect to be surprised by what is invented.

These innovations can help solve specific BOP customer challenges, and can be designed to the variability of each market segment. Because the global water crisis is not a crisis in the same way, in all places, for all people, we must collect real data on how BOP customers think, live, organize, and work. Some customers may have access to clean water, but it's too far from their homes, unreliable, or exorbitantly expensive; others may have no access at all. Urban dwellers might want a loan to pay for a household utility connection. Rainwater harvesting tanks can benefit residents of countries with consistent rains, but a bore well might better serve rural communities in arid regions.

Traditional return-on-investment metrics—health outcomes, school days gained, and so on—remain worthy pulse points for communities and charitable activity. But for this next wave of innovation, a new set of metrics will factor in market forces to measure catalytic impact, with the specific goal of measuring growing consumer heft—for example, the amount of social or commercial capital that has been leveraged, and whether the philanthropic cost per person reached is diminishing. Though clean water for everyone is the clear goal, we need a secondary one as well: As a sector we should be working to put ourselves out of business. And by seeding a marketplace with a soul, we can do just that.

THE OPPORTUNITY AHEAD:
FAMILIAR CHOKEPOINTS AND ORTHOGONAL FORCES

Water.org's experience working on the ground with people who face the water crisis daily has revealed the sector's biggest obstacles as a series of market failures and an overall lack of accountability on the part of governments and utilities. These chokepoints yield a highly dysfunctional system that deters the very civic, social, and commercial capital investments needed to jump-start widespread progress. Without intervention, the sector will continue to limp along with sporadic infusions of international aid, charity, and investments on the part of governments and the development banks.

By systematically attacking the twin chokepoints of market failures and accountability, we can start a ripple effect that will drive system change and create a world in which everyone can meet their basic water needs. The chokepoints are not new. What is new, however, are models of financing and advances in technology that have fostered a democratization of information and capital, with the potential to change the rules of the entire game.

Moreover, seemingly unrelated (orthogonal) forces also have the potential to inspire innovation that can attract the needed capital and spur greater accountability. Other sectors have begun to apply new approaches, and the water and sanitation sectors can learn from and leverage their experiences. New perspectives and trends have informed this analysis and proposed solutions, and hold great promise for accelerating the pace of progress.

MARKET FAILURES AND NEW FINANCING MODELS

New models of financing are encouraging NGOs and donors to get smarter about how they use capital, seeking efficiencies that have eluded us for decades. These new models of financing are being driven at least in part by the proliferation of catalytic philanthropy by individuals and foundations. This philanthropic capital is distinguishable from traditional charity by the expectations of investors to see how their dollars are seeding market development so that one day their philanthropy no longer will be needed for the positive change to continue occurring and even grow. Approaches such as microfinance are good examples of this in action. With strategic grant investments (typically made years earlier), microfinance institutions have been able to grow, thereby making capital available to those living in poverty, opening up entirely new markets to previously marginalized individuals. Similarly, pooling grant capital into advanced market commitments has successfully jump-started markets—as in the case of vaccines against pneumococcal disease—and reassured private-sector investors and industry of the return on their investment.

To bring safe water to every citizen of the world, we need more and better capital on a scale available only from commercial markets. The only way to attract that capital is with economic efficiency. Poorly targeted, supply-driven solutions, such as the charitable model for mitigating the water crisis, tend to fuel inefficiency and stymie efficiencies inherent to a demand-driven market. We know that people in developing countries are not uniformly poor and that there's money to be spent; shifting to a demand-driven model is a clear way to better serve more customers and to ensure that enough charity is available for the absolute poor, who desperately need a direct subsidy.

In Her Own Words

I am Mrs. Kolanchi, residing at Kamaraj Nagar of Ariyamangalam Zone in Trichy City Corporation in India. I am forty-seven years old and my husband passed away over a year ago. I have three sons and three daughters.

We have suffered a lot because of poverty. All of my children discontinued their studies and went to work jobs instead to support the family. Because we all work, we don't get adequate water for our needs because the public water supply is usually collected from six A.M. to eight A.M. in our area. More than one hundred people collect water from that single tap. People even fight among themselves while collecting the water. I work in a hotel and return home at midnight but because water collection is in the early hours, we would wake up early in the morning with hardly any sleep to wait at the public tap to collect water. It greatly affected our livelihood activities. Day after day this continued and I became sick because of this difficult situation.

At this time, Mrs. Bagyalakshmi of Kamaraj Nagar told me about Water.org and Guardian (a local Water.org partner) working in our area and providing loans for water and sanitation. Upon hearing this I joined a joint lending group and received a loan for a water connection. Now I have water right in my home and it is no problem for me to collect it! There are families like me who also suffer a lot because of water. I have asked Guardian to identify them and also help them address their water needs.

ACCOUNTABILITY
AND TECHNOLOGY

Transparency is a precursor for accountability, and better accountability can help address inequities and inefficiencies in water's many delivery systems, improving services and bolstering investor confidence. Billions of dollars are spent annually on water infrastructure and services, yet approximately half of the money is lost due to fraud, mismanagement, and lack of proper operation and maintenance. Advances in information and communication technology could improve accountability and empower poor individuals and communities.

Mobile and web technologies are now widely accessible to some of the poorest people in the world. These technologies are uniquely suited to increase accountability because they can enable almost real-time investment tracking, information dissemination to even the most marginalized populations, and participation from many previously disenfranchised groups. Many development sectors are already using global positioning system (GPS) technology, text messaging, and social media to raise funds, report to donors, and increase awareness. These technologies can also directly benefit clients, for example, by alerting mothers to the schedule for a mobile immunization clinic, or informing fishermen of market prices so they can receive a fair wholesale price for their catch.

There are clear opportunities to push out information to the citizenry, information such as water investments earmarked for underserved communities in rural, urban, or peri-urban areas and the status of those initiatives. Citizens need access to this kind of information to begin to hold their leaders accountable. Mobile technology also can deliver real-time access to the locations, status, and prices of water supplies from public taps, tanker trucks, and water kiosks. These seemingly simple interventions could prevent price gouging by unscrupulous vendors, save individuals weeks of lost annual productivity spent scavenging for water, and empower communities to hold their leaders and service providers accountable for improvements that are never completed or funds that seep through cracks in the system. Application of technology can help the poor to leverage their power as customers and citizens, and find their voice in demanding better water services in much the same way the Arab Spring helped people find their political voice—and Water.org is helping people organize themselves, for example, through the women's self-help groups that take out WaterCredit loans.

"CROWD-SOURCING" IDEAS AND CREATING A SPACE FOR INNOVATION

To take advantage of opportunities such as microfinance and mobile technology—and to discover new opportunities—we can challenge ourselves and the sector at large to look beyond our traditional boundaries and invite in new thinkers and ideas.

System-changing solutions like those proposed require a paradigm shift. We must reach past our assumptions, past what we perceive to be best practices, and even past the parameters of the water or development sector. We need to create an ecosystem in which people from seemingly unrelated sectors can convene, generate new ideas, foster fledgling ideas, and reassess and hone those ideas that have the greatest potential to drive system change. The world doesn't need another working group or an entity to codify best practices or define sustainability, and these ideas must have life beyond a flip chart or white paper. In this new ecosystem, this "liquid network," thinkers and doers from a wide range of sectors and industries can convene to identify and explore orthogonal forces, to capitalize on emerging ideas, and to reinspire one another and our shared vision.

Applied Inspiration

The Clinton Global Initiative, the Hult International Business School, and Water.org jointly issued a global challenge in early spring 2011 to generate game-changing ideas to benefit those at the base of the economic pyramid who lack safe water and sanitation. Hundreds of business students representing more than 130 countries—many of which struggle with the very water crisis we've examined in this chapter—generated solutions to help alleviate the crisis. Thirty panels of judges in five regional competitions (Shanghai, Dubai, London, Boston, and San Francisco) narrowed the field to five teams that competed at the global final, hosted by Water.org, Hult, and former president Bill Clinton, in the spring of 2011. Water.org is now mining these ideas with the goal of piloting new initiatives the water sector may never have conceived of without outside inspiration.

A CALL TO ACTION

Everyone in the world deserves sustainable and affordable access to safe water. Fundamental system change is the only way to make this happen—change driven by the intrinsic power of the poor as customers and citizens. We must use innovative financing models and technology to address the twin chokepoints of market efficiency and accountability to correct the flawed system that has limited large-scale and lasting solutions to the water crisis. Although we should take a long-term view in this regard, we should not discount the role of subsidized interventions, when properly targeted, or interim solutions such as private sector vendors, when scrupulous, until utilities can be expanded to poor neighborhoods. The world in which we operate will always require some level of subsidy for the absolute poor, but innovations in financing can more effectively direct those subsidies to the people who need them most.

No single group or sector holds all the answers. We all should fully expect to refine and recalibrate our approaches drawing on the ideas and experiences of others, but we must remain aware that there's no time to waste. A water shortage is in the offing for the United States and other developed countries, but it has already reached crisis proportions for more vulnerable communities in the developing world. As the global outlook grows more serious, the world's poor will see their situation deteriorate even more rapidly than those living in industrialized countries.

We're calling on water and sanitation experts and novices alike. We're calling on leaders in technology, economics, and civil society. We're calling on innovative philanthropists, engineers, writers, and thinkers. We're calling on everyone to join together to spur innovation, catalyze capital, and drive transparency and accountability. Lend your voice as an advocate on behalf of those in need. Build on the growing awareness of the global water crisis, and help create a movement that mobilizes leaders, resources, and transformative innovation.

By unleashing the power of the poor we will ensure that everyone in the world can take a safe drink of water in our lifetime.

8

DRAWING WATER

Soft-Path Thinking and Drylands Design

Hadley Arnold and Peter Arnold

Hadley Arnold and Peter Arnold are codirectors of the Arid Lands Institute (ALI) at Woodbury University in Burbank, California, an innovative education, outreach, and applied research center. ALI serves as both a training ground for the next generation of water-smart design leaders and a nonprofit planning and design-advisory firm, rethinking the West's urban, rural, and suburban water needs. Fieldwork, multidisciplinary seminars, and architecture, landscape, and urban design studios are organized around contracted work with partner communities. Student-faculty teams work together to generate both progressive design proposals and actionable policy recommendations. Although the focus of the work is the US West, ALI continually asks: How are water-smart design proposals for the West exportable, scalable, and replicable to drylands globally?

When ALI and its collaborators talk about retrofitting the West in the face of water scarcity and hydrologic variability brought on by climate change, the "soft path" is often cited as the antidote to the "hard path" of massive engineering infrastructures that shape both the West's water systems and the West's agricultural and urban economies. But when we talk about the "soft path of water" at ALI, we both reference and depart from customary usage.

Amory Lovins coined the term "soft path" in the 1970s to differentiate energy conservation and efficiency measures as a form of "supply" distinct from those that depend on massive concentrations of capital, technology, and power—the "hard path"—to extract and deliver resources. The soft path depends instead on the low-hanging fruit of conservation achieved through adjusting existing technologies and users' behaviors.

In this century, Peter Gleick of the Pacific Institute uses the term as it applies to water conservation. In considering California's urban water use, for example, "soft path" implies using automated sprinklers, taking shorter showers, requiring low-flush toilets, and following low-impact development guidelines. Compared with massive new supply infrastructures or developing new technologies, soft path measures are fast, cheap, and highly effective—for example, even after three decades of significant population increase, Los Angeles today uses water at levels that are roughly the same as those prevalent in 1979, thanks largely to the use of mandated low-flush toilets. But the path of conservation is not the soft path we are talking about, and not the one in which we as designers are most interested.

Arguably, a soft path that focuses on specifying water-efficient fixtures and water-conserving behaviors renders design of the built environment impotent and inconsequential, just as the hard path of engineering centralized infrastructures does. In both cases, the design of space, buildings, and landscapes essentially *doesn't matter.* When the heavy lifting of negotiating the relationship between natural resources and the built environment is done by other instruments—capital, energy, policy, or plumbing (large or small)—design atrophies, rendered irrelevant as a tool for negotiating the right relationship with place and neighbor.

For us the soft path, more fruitfully drawn, is the path of water itself—a path that follows water's own logic, the path of least resistance. The medium is not technology, either large (centralized engineering) or small (carefully specified fixtures). The medium is space: infrastructural space, urban space, landscape space, and architectural space, conceived not technologically, but hydrologically. ALI reasserts the shaping of form and space as society's principal tools for adapting to the changing hydrologic cycle.

Rather than frame the West's water challenges and the possible solutions in terms of "the technology of water capture," our focus is instead "the recapture of water logic." We say "recapture" rather than "invention" because we are the first society in history to have divorced—indeed, actively defied, forgotten, or attempted to erase—the logic of water from the layout of our settlements, the shape of our civic life, the design of our public architectures, the disposition of our domestic spaces, and the functioning of our fields. The twentieth-century development of the western United States occurred at just the right place (a sparsely populated half continent) and just the right time (access to federal capital, political will, and cheap energy) to divorce volume from efficiency, citizen from governance, cognition from use, and sanctity from utility.

Recapturing a grammar of drylands design—reinvesting the human-altered surfaces of the West with the logic of water—is ALI's true goal, the next generation of western designers' most powerful technology, and potentially design's most important contribution to a durable human future.

SNOW, RAIN, AND THE DESIGN LOGIC OF THE ARID WEST: PROBLEMS AND OPPORTUNITIES

Water and energy. To recover a logic of drylands design, one first would need to contend with the ill logic of some current systems. Hard-path engineering has constructed a western surface—from the dams, reservoirs, and aqueducts of the Great Basin and the Sierra

Nevada to the pitched roofs, gutters, curbs, and storm drains of paved Los Angeles, Phoenix, Tucson, Las Vegas, San Diego, and Denver—designed to do two things: deliver us snowmelt and rid us of storm water.

Dependence on long-distance imported water (snowmelt) and rapid discarding of local water (storm water) is the fundamental condition of the West's single-grade, single-use water logic. Its working is predicated on access to cheap, plentiful energy. If there is one thing to "get" about the contemporary condition of western water, its hard-path logic, and the working of the contemporary western economy, it is simply this equation:

$$\text{West} = \text{Water} + \text{Energy}$$

The built, farmed, and altered landscapes of the West depend heavily on carbon-intensive energy for water extraction, distribution, use, treatment, and disposal. This water-energy nexus means that it takes a lot of water to make energy, and it takes a lot of energy to use water. And it takes a lot of both to run a major modern economy in a water-scarce environment.

To put this nexus in perspective, the extraction, treatment, distribution, use, and disposal of water require approximately 8 percent of the nation's energy.[1] That figure skews dramatically higher as one moves westward. Lifting snowmelt out of rivers and delivering it across deserts and mountains takes an extreme amount of energy. Thus, water's extraction, treatment, distribution, use, and disposal require 20 percent of California's electricity and 30 percent of California's natural gas.[2] The largest buyer of electricity in California

---

1 *Water's Links to Energy and Greenhouse Gases*, Northern Colorado Industrial, Commercial, and Institutional Water Conservation Collaboration, December 2007.

2 R. Cohen, B. Nelson, and G. Wolff, "Energy Down the Drain: The Hidden Costs of California's Water Supply," Natural Resources Defense Council, Oakland, California, 2004, www.nrdc.org/water/conservation/edrain/execsum.asp.

is the State of California—to operate the State Water Project, delivering northern Sierra snowmelt to Southern California, over the Tehachapi Mountains. The second-largest buyer of electricity in California is the Metropolitan Water District—to operate the Colorado River Aqueduct, delivering Rocky Mountain snowmelt to Southern California, across the Mojave.

Although California's power is 46 percent natural gas–driven and 20 percent nuclear, the state buys a significant portion of its electricity from the coal-driven western utility grid. California's share alone in western coal plants releases 67 million tons of global-warming carbon dioxide—equivalent to emissions from one car for each of greater LA's 11 million residents. The population of metropolitan Tucson, Arizona, is 1 million. The energy required per year just to bring water via the Central Arizona Project to those 1 million is equivalent to the energy required per year to heat, cool, and light 52 million average American homes.

And just as western water depends on large concentrations of energy, energy production in the West is water-intensive. Nationwide the power-generating sector uses approximately one-third of the nation's developed water resources. Coal-fired plants use 510 gallons per megawatt-hour of energy produced; natural gas plants, 415 gallons; the cooling processes of nuclear plants use 785 gallons of water per megawatt-hour of energy produced; producing one gallon of ethanol requires 1,000 gallons of water; hydroelectric plants, due to their high rates of reservoir evaporation, use 30,000 gallons of water per megawatt-hour of energy produced. Palo Verde, the nation's largest nuclear plant, located in Arizona, uses more than 20 billion gallons of water annually for cooling purposes. Navajo and Four Corners, both coal-driven, each use 8 billion gallons a year for cooling. Together that's equivalent to the water used by 640,000 people for a year, at current LA usage rates.

So rule number one of a recaptured water logic for design in drylands must be: *Mitigate the rate and scope of water's role in a carbon-based economy.* No "water solution" for the US West (or any-where) is a true solution unless it is also an energy solution.

A snowmelt-driven society in a desert powered by carbon is a design laid out in plan, with the inconvenience of gravity overcome by adding energy. A grammar of carbon-free drylands design sug-gests not just a shift to alternative energy sources, but the refusal to use added energy; that we use, wherever possible, the logic of gravity to guide design. Think like a raindrop; think like a watershed, think like physics: all water wants to do is go down. Water will show you its own soft path—the literal path of least resistance. Make use of it along the way. Think in section. Uncouple the water-energy nexus.

Water and variability. Grasping the connection between western water and western energy requires us to make the connection be-tween our current hydraulics and climate change. Water, energy use, and heat-trapping greenhouse gas emissions are, as Peter Gleick has worked hard to show, "directly related, and self-limiting." Simply put in western terms:

$$\text{More } H_2O = \text{More } CO_2; \text{More } CO_2 = \text{Less } H_2O$$

It's not that there will actually be less H_2O in a climate-changed West; more accurately, it will be allocated differently, in a way that makes it increasingly difficult to capture, store, and use. More pre-cipitation is projected to fall as rain instead of snow, increasing seasonal storm-water flooding, and snowpack will melt earlier, di-minishing late spring runoff. That's hydrologic variability. Water supplies that are highly variable are less manageable. The problem is different from scarcity, but either way we're not ready for it. The capture and harvest of local waters (meaning, in a land of overdrawn groundwater, rainwater, storm water, gray water, and wastewater) will be both more difficult than managing slow-release snow, and more critical. Native waters will spike in value as imports grow less reliable as the sole source for sustaining a growing population.

Twentieth-century hard-path system design relied on stationarity—
the notion that natural systems fluctuate within an unchanging en-
velope that can be described, modeled, and predicted.[3] But
mounting scientific evidence documents a rapidly changing hydrological regime in the western United States.[4] The current approach
is failing.[5] As Milly et al. boldly declared in *Science* in 2008, "Stationarity is dead." Variability—the result of a reallocated hydrologic
cycle brought on by climate change—requires new ways of thinking.
Fixed, centralized, overscaled, and energy-intensive infrastructures;
impermeable urbanisms; artificially supported architectures; and
the hydrologic models upon which they were based, and the policies
that uphold them—all these are obsolete.

Hence, water-logic rule number two: *Adapt to regional climate-
change impacts; anticipate the certain or near-certain changes in the
hydrologic cycle already under way.*

Captured rainwater, storm-water runoff, gray water, and wastewater combined form the West's largest undeveloped water supply.
Opportunistically exploiting this supply will require, at every scale,
an inversion of the usual order of things: flood as opportunity; surface as sponge; roof as cup; waste as sustenance; city as farm. Each
physical surface, vertical and horizontal, of the built environment
will require a dual character: rapid saturation and slow release; plentiful storage and disciplined consumption; fat and lean; wet and dry.
Design for variability.

---

3   P. C. D. Milly, Julio Betancourt, Malin Falkenmark, Robert M. Hirsch, Zbigniew W.
Kundzewicz, Dennis P. Lettenmaier, and Ronald J. Stouffer, "Stationarity Is Dead: Whither
Water Management?" *Science* 319 (February 1, 2008).

4   J. H. Christensen et al., "Regional Climate Projections," in *Climate Change 2007: The
Physical Science Basis*, ed. S. Solomon et al. (Cambridge: Cambridge University Press,
2007).

5   Peter H. Gleick, "Roadmap for Sustainable Water Resources in Southwestern North
America," *Proceedings of the National Academy of Sciences* 107, no. 50 (December 14, 2010):
21301.

WATER AND LOCAL IDENTITY

Burbank, California, as case study in emergent drylands design. What does a western community retooled according to the primary logic of water look like? We're not sure, but a multiyear partnership with the City of Burbank, California, funded by the federal department of Housing and Urban Development gives us an opportunity to explore possibilities.

A foothill city of 100,000 in the Upper Los Angeles River Watershed, Burbank serves as a test bed for progressive drylands design thinking. Like most of the West, it is engineered to shed local, carbon-free water and import remote, energy-intensive water. Like most of Southern California, its local groundwater resources are in overdraft and have been for decades. Unlike many western cities, however, Burbank has identified water capture as a critical priority.

Burbank's emphasis on aquifer recharge is not driven so much by an aspiration to relocalize supply as by the need to remediate a local groundwater contamination problem. Burbank's aquifer has been a designated federal Superfund site since the 1980s: industrial contaminants including trichloroethylene (TCE), perchloroethylene (PCE), and chromium-6 permeate it, a legacy of the midcentury aerospace industry. For twenty-five years, the city's critical water objective has been to dilute the aquifer to treatable levels. Working with the federal Environmental Protection Agency, the city has made tremendous progress in diluting the contaminants.

However, water illogics of the US West compound the task: clean water brought to Burbank from the Sierras and the Rockies is used to dilute a contaminated aquifer. Diluted contaminated water is then withdrawn for treatment and use. Policy hardens the arteries of illogic: no groundwater recharge credits are extended to Burbank for placing (free, carbon-neutral) local storm water into the aquifer; Burbank receives credit only for recharging the aquifer using imported water. Not unlike a dysfunctional health-care scenario, this might be equivalent to prescribing expensive medications with known side effects to treat a condition that exercise would benefit—and simultaneously prohibiting exercise.

While making strong (if convoluted) progress on aquifer reme-diation, Burbank has also emerged as a water-recycling leader in the United States, recycling 8 percent of municipal wastewater supplies. Although 8 percent may not sound like much, it places not far behind the world's second–most efficient water recycler, Spain, which re-claims 12 percent of municipal wastewater. (Israel shames us all, how-ever, recycling 75 percent of its supply.) A limited market for its product, however, hampers Burbank's leadership as a water recycler. Though some of Burbank's recycled water is pumped to a public golf course for irrigation, 7 million gallons of high-grade recycled waste-water are released each day to the Western Channel, joining the Los Angeles River and flowing to Long Beach. Recycled wastewater in Burbank meets important water quality objectives—treated water flowing to the ocean is better than untreated water, certainly—but misses the opportunity to offset critical water supply challenges.

At the same time that Burbank's water managers are progressing on diluting the aquifer (though with energy-intensive water imports) and recycling urban wastewater (though releasing most of it down-stream), city planners are responding to the requirements of Cali-fornia's aggressive climate change mitigation law, Assembly Bill 32 (AB32), passed in 2006. This law committed California to reducing greenhouse gas emissions to 1990 levels by 2020, a reduction of ap-proximately 30 percent from business-as-usual projections. On a per capita basis, this is equivalent to reducing annual emissions from 14 tons of CO_2E (carbon dioxide equivalent) per person in Califor-nia to about 10 tons per person by 2020.

Like most planning offices in the state, Burbank's is focusing its AB32-mandated climate action plan on transportation and compact development—reducing vehicle miles traveled in an auto-centric culture. By point-of-use accounting methods, water simply does not account for enough of Burbank's energy footprint to warrant serious consideration as a tool to reduce greenhouse gas emissions; emissions associated with water use in Burbank are calculated by planners and consultants at less than 2 percent of the city's total emissions (even though one-fifth of the state's energy is used to deliver that water).

So, in Burbank, as in most western cities, water remains isolated from energy, design of the built environment, and climate change mitigation objectives. However, a number of factors, including progressive leadership in public office and public utilities and a committed core of volunteer citizen leaders, suggest that integration of water, energy, and climate change objectives are not far off in Burbank.

Our hope and our claim is that design, beginning with the visual synthesis of data, the mapping and modeling of existing conditions, and the identification of strategic opportunities for intervention, can help catalyze that integration by projecting the vision of a landscape of abundant possibility. That's the work in which ALI is now engaged.

Our design work began with analytic mapping of water and energy flows at several scales: the scale of regional systems (water imports), the scale of the hydrologic basin (local groundwater flows), and the scale of land use (surface water, permeability, and stormwater and wastewater flows). ALI teams have extensively mapped and modeled the historical behaviors of the natural watershed and the contemporary functioning of the synthetic watershed. These models identify the strategic opportunities for capturing groundwater at the scale of the watershed and surface water and wastewater at the scale of land uses within municipal boundaries. One goal was to generate a menu of strategies that translate potential water harvests into energy offsets and climate mitigation strategies.

Using "true cost" accounting methods developed by Robert C. Wilkinson, director of the Water Policy Program, Bren School of

Environmental Science and Management at the University of California at Santa Barbara, ALI teams calculated energy associated with Burbank's water and translated it into household use as measured in terms of compact fluorescent lightbulbs. We found that Burbank's water energy could light a 750-square-mile territory, twenty-four hours a day. Recalibrating water's energy gives planners another tool for achieving climate action objectives. If you offset water imports with local water, how greatly could you accelerate the process of attaining 1990 greenhouse gas emission levels? A preliminary study quantifies maximum potential for storm-water harvest and suggests a potential runoff harvest in Burbank equal to 5,776 acre-feet. If, at current usage rates, one acre-foot—approximately 325,000 gallons—supplies one year of water for 6.5 Burbank residents, then this is enough water for 37,500 Burbank residents—or one-third of the population—for a year. And that saving occurs *without* conservation measures in place.

To translate (in an oversimplification, with no accounting for treatment costs) that water/energy opportunity into the terms of a climate action plan: if these 5,776 acre-feet of local (low-energy, low-carbon) water offset the water imported from remote sources, it would amount to a potential energy savings of 22,217,243 kilowatt-hours. At 8,000 kilowatt-hours per capita per year as a California average, that is the equivalent of offsetting the energy of 2,800 residents' annual domestic electricity usage. In tons of CO_2E, it's the equivalent of just under 9,000 pickup trucks.

Beyond providing a rationale for why a western city like Burbank might undertake a hydraulic retrofit, ALI's challenge is to provide a vision for where and how. By modeling the water and energy inputs specific to each land use, each economic sector, each block, we could see the relative cost-benefit ratio of targeting specific surface areas for localized water capture rather than importation. The most striking opportunities were from 80 percent to 100 percent impermeability zones—largely industrial—with a complementary approach to green streets and alleys, using Burbank Water and Power design guidelines already in place. The impermeability zones targeted as potential storm-water harvest and aquifer recharge sites corresponded closely to the city's economic development zones, suggesting opportunities for leveraged investment into natural systems infrastructure in these areas.

Next we identified commercial parking lots, schoolyards, and public parks as clear targets for permeable retrofits that could be cross-programmed to perform multiple functions as localized hydraulic infrastructure integrated with public space.

A third sector ripe for intervention, basic to reengineering the essential DNA of the waterlogged western city, consists of single-family dwellings and the low-density neighborhoods they make up. And here a host of exciting and potentially revolutionary questions await us.

With irrigation of private property the single biggest user of Burbank's water budget (close to 50 percent), what is the fate of—or the alternative to—the iconic American lawn? With pitched roofs and graded sites sheeting water, by law, off-site as quickly as possible, one must equally ask: What is the fate of—or alternative to—the existing construction conventions and building codes? What if water systems become drivers of both site design and building form? What if roof becomes catchment, cistern becomes structural, wall sections distributive? What if wet elements of an architectural program are sequenced according to a logic of gravity? What if building systems are organized around multiple gradations of water rather than using water with the universal grade of "potable" to wash our cars, flush our toilets, and water our gardens? What if "hard" enclosed spaces are closely interlocked with a micronetwork of "soft" passive treatment landscapes? Can the much-revered California integration of indoor and outdoor life be blurred further, not just artfully but fruitfully?

Answering these and many related questions will take time. Work is ongoing between Burbank and ALI. For us as designers, this is where the fun begins—with our conviction that these questions have possible, valid answers in reconfigured forms, spaces, materials, and the behaviors they shape, rather than in pricing policy or piping projects.

It has been said that the three possible human responses to climate change, in competing scenarios and varying combinations, are mitigation (slow it down), adaptation (evolve to fit it), and dislocation (suffering of the most vulnerable). Perhaps design has a wedge it can jam in the door of suffering. If collaborators can exploit the inventory of local assets as abundant design opportunity, and invest in the quirks and peculiarities of scarce local resources and design the buildings that most fully capitalize on them, the resulting radical dislocation from business as usual might serve as a source of creative transformation, particular to place and people.

Here, then, is water logic rule number three for the design of adaptation: *Celebrate the particulars of local identity and design into the fringes of existing constraints. Take risk, get peculiar.*

As in biology, diversification of our built environment's gene pool enhances our capacity for resilience in the face of change and increases our "fitness" for our environment. In the design of adaptation, monocultures have no place. Design for multiple waters and many Wests. Resequence. Cross over. Mutate. Diversify. Select for beneficial advantages. Evolve.

CREATING SOCIAL EQUITY: DESIGN BEYOND MEASURE

ALI is joining with creative thinkers, designers, decision makers, educators, and citizens all over the West to ask: Can future infrastructures, rural and urban, be redesigned to address storm water as resource and flood events as opportunities? Can existing flood control structures be retooled to slow, store, and distribute useable agricultural and/or municipal water? Can water extraction, treatment, distribution, use, and disposal shift to localized control and low-carbon energy sources and continue to meet the demands of a growing population? How might multifunctional, self-regulating, locally managed infrastructures, surgically implanted into existing landscapes and neighborhoods, attract investment, sustain economies, and promote ecological stability? Can such shifts occur at effective scales, and at a sufficiently rapid pace, to meet the challenge of decelerating climate change?

All of these functions have quantifiable measures of success, described in gallons, acre-feet, people, households, tons of CO_2E, dollars, jobs, and so on. They are difficult to define precisely (numbers are as manipulatable as words), and the obstacles to achieving them are significant. For example, there are persistent impediments to transforming storm-water management, groundwater recharge, and wastewater recycling policy, including a lack of understanding of performance and cost implications, a lack of integrated policy approaches and legislative mandates, a lack of communication between the scientific/engineering/design communities and policy makers, and general resistance to change.[6] Design alone won't overcome any of these impediments, especially considering the jurisdictional complexity that is a distinguishing feature of the West's contested water landscape. More than forty federal, state, regional, and local agencies share responsibility for western water policy.[7]

---

6 Allison H. Roy et al., "Impediments and Solutions to Sustainable, Watershed-Scale Urban Stormwater Management: Lessons from Australia and the United States," *Environmental Management* 42 (April 30, 2008): 344–359; Katherine Jacobs, former director, Arizona Water Institute, in prepared remarks, Climate Change Conference, Water Education Foundation, Long Beach, California, November 13, 2008; and Roy et al., "Impediments and Solutions."

7 Gleick, "Roadmap for Sustainable Water Resources," 21304.

Beyond these humbling and elusive "hard" measures, however, are others. They might be described as "softer" in that they are less precisely described, but they also may be described as "harder" in that they are even more difficult to attain. The greatest potential in the critique of hard-path thinking lies outside the quantifiable. It lies in the requirement to think, and design, beyond instrumentalism. Neither using less water nor securing more is the central goal of a deeply intelligent environmental design. The soft path of water asks us qualitative questions about built form and civic life; about the body, sensual, social, and politic; about cultural identity and the role of ritual, quotidian and festive, in a pluralistic society; about our relationship to water as biological sacrament. Can redesigned water systems not only power an engine of local civic engagement but also powerfully reawaken our sensory engagement with our environment? Can distributed water networks be designed not only to be socially and ecologically careful, but to re-enchant everyday life as well? Can a water system's beauty interrupt ignorance or arrest apathy? Can a system's transparency trigger cognition, rewiring a lost link between user and source? Can the full expressive potential of water-smart architecture recalibrate not only the volume of water a community uses but also the character of that community's relationship to the natural world? Can water, and the contemplation of its absence, be visibly reintroduced into the poetic nature of the arid and semiarid city form?

To shape public life, carry cultural values, and inform everyday experience, from utilitarian to sacral, is what drylands water infrastructures have always done, from Yazd to Fez, Istanbul to Rome, from Avestan's *pairidaēza* to Andalusia's Alhambra, from the *chinampas* of the Aztecs to the acequias of the Rio Embudo and the *zanja madre* of El Pueblo de Nuestra Señora de Los Angeles de Porciúncula. Do we still know how to create such infrastructures?

ALI is as invested in the qualitative outcome of better water system design as it is in the quantitative, as concerned with the soft measures as the hard, and we draw our inspiration from our commitment to history as much as we do from our commitment to the future. ALI is Janus-faced: We look both inward to local and regional, and outward to global precedents and applications. We look backward to history as much as forward to our students' and our children's inheritance. We are, in some ways, still responding to pioneering conservationist John Wesley Powell's persuasive plea. In his 1878 *Report on the Lands of the Arid Regions,* Powell argued that a hydrographic redrawing of the West could serve as an intelligent basis for ordering settlement and managing scarce resources dynamically. The irregular—and by Enlightenment standards, rather backward—geometry of watershed delineation could, he argued, serve as the basic unit for shaping a land-based democracy of informed, self-governing citizens, responsive to the particulars of local conditions. Merely extending the Euclidian grid of the land ordinances across a half continent where water resources were so inequitably distributed would drain that grid of its radical and rationalist promise of an equal shot at a competent, informed, land-based prosperity for all. Instead, Powell argued, we could redraw the geometry and deliver on the Jeffersonian promise. But if we kept the Jeffersonian geometry, we would have to artificially support it with hydraulic engineering beyond the capabilities of local governance. The result: a federalized landscape rather than a localized one; concentration of power rather than distribution of opportunity.

The critical historians of the West—Bernard de Voto, Wallace Stegner, Donald Worster, Charles Bowden, Marc Reisner, Gerald Nash, Morris Hundley, and others—have looked hard at the ideological relationship between hard-path water infrastructure and the centralization of social and economic power. As they have well argued in compelling and lyric narrative, the infrastructure of a federalized landscape and a hydraulic empire promises us comfort, convenience, and prosperity in the near term, and in return asks us to surrender responsibility for our own future. The infrastructure of empire spawns biological and social monoculture: water and the West are rendered placeless, historyless, barren. A geography mythologized for its rugged self-reliance, they have powerfully argued, is engineered instead for dependence, stagnation, and a brittle vulnerability to change.

A new grammar of drylands design—variable, flexible, recombinant, responsive to local culture, values, habitat, and climate—is a tool for ecological health. But better yet, as Powell provokes us to consider, it's a tool for ideological health. Only a society—or a constellation of multiple cultures—of competent citizen-stewards embracing creative adaptation, resourcefulness, and self-management is worthy of the myth of the West as true testing ground of the American experiment. Powell's argument that we should shed the neat emerald-green grid of the lily-white East to settle the West on its own terms echoes prophetically across economic, ecological, and ethnic divides today. It is time, Powell might argue, that the West gets comfortable living in its dusty-brown skin.

Before Stegner and De Voto, before Powell's report and Jefferson's *Farm Book,* others wrote of the hard work of the soft path, and the full ideological implications of drawing one's own water. Herodotus, in the *Ninth Book of the Histories,* challenges us from Halicarnassus in the fifth century BCE: "It is better, to live in a rugged land and rule than to cultivate rich plains and be subject to others."

Hence recovered water logic rule number four: *Design for a rugged land.*

9

FROM CRISIS TO COMPETITIVE ADVANTAGE

How Businesses Are Learning Sustainable Water Management

Robyn Beavers

Robyn Beavers became a pioneer in the clean technologies and sustainability movement while an undergraduate in civil engineering at Stanford University, when she organized a campus-wide for-credit seminar on clean technologies. After graduating with an engineering degree, Beavers worked for an energy efficiency consulting firm based in the San Francisco Bay Area. In 2004 she joined Google, where she worked directly for the two founders as their leader for establishing sustainability and clean energy programs within the company. After five years, Beavers left Google to study at the Stanford Graduate School of Business, where she earned an MBA. After her graduate studies, Beavers moved to Europe to join the global marketing team at the headquarters of Vestas Wind Systems, the second-largest maker of wind turbines in the world.

I have always considered myself an optimist; I tend to think of a partially filled glass of water as being half full rather than half empty. However, as I have learned more about the business of water and how it is shaping our global economy, I have also learned that nature and humanity are in a growing struggle about how to use water, take care of it, and carefully distribute it—a struggle that is approaching a crisis point.

The optimist in me allows me to see the opportunities that exist and to see how the growing problems can be solved with enlightened management, with careful attention to important facts about the true value of water, and with the deployment of a variety of proven and emerging technologies. Thankfully, this type of thinking and the behavior that should naturally follow are beginning to appear in the business world. More and more businesses are learning that sustainability makes good business sense and that the growing crisis in water is not only a call to action but also an opportunity to innovate. The markets they serve will tell them whether they are successful and whether they are moving in the right direction.

In the next few pages, I'll share some of the events that helped me develop a more acute sense of the water crisis from a pragmatic business perspective. I'll also outline some of the opportunities that exist for dealing with this crisis, along with examples of companies that are learning that sustainable water management is not only an essential economic need but an opportunity for competitive advantage as well.

WATER FROM A CORPORATE SUSTAINABILITY PERSPECTIVE

My interest in sustainability started with my love of buildings, which developed during my civil engineering studies. It became clear to me that in the future our buildings, which are such an integral part of our life on Earth, could be designed to be so much better. Buildings could be designed to be healthy and more efficient. Buildings could become living systems that did not just protect their inhabitants from the exterior climate but also created an interior space that people wanted to occupy. My interest in sustainable buildings caused me to start my career focused on energy.

My professional roles have allowed me to spend my time designing and implementing tangible projects that either reduced the amount of energy required to perform the same amount of work or generated power in a renewable and environmentally friendly way. The renewable energy projects I've worked on have produced easily measurable financial benefits through the right balance of existing or emerging technologies and solutions that were becoming available at industrial scale. But success didn't always come easy. To deliver real results, I just had to roll up my sleeves, convince a few of the right people that change can be good, and push the projects through.

One project that I proposed, planned, and managed through installation at Google headquarters was the largest and most cost-effective (as of 2006) nongovernment solar power system in the country, using over 9,700 photovoltaic panels with a combined output of 1.6 megawatts.

During my graduate studies, which were designed around becoming a leader in financially sound sustainability practices, I realized it was time for me to really understand what the water crisis was all about. Like many people, I knew water was an important resource that was becoming scarcer, but I was not really clear about what that meant. I assumed that learning about water would be similar and complementary to my education about energy. After all, water, like energy, was a measurable resource with a price assigned to it. Water was probably used inefficiently so things could be designed to use less of it. And there were probably ways to produce clean water more easily and efficiently than in the past. An analogous set of questions for clean energy had been asked and answered over the past decade, so it seemed likely that water could follow suit.

However, it soon became clear to me that the study of water came with a new set of questions that demanded new answers. I realized that water was something more than a cheap commodity that flowed into a building through one pipe and flowed out of the building through another.

I learned the distinction between "big water" and "small water." By "big water" I mean the natural cycle of water evaporating from lakes and oceans, falling to Earth as rain, and then creating underground aquifers or flowing across the land into streams and rivers. Over the ages, mankind has built massive projects that divert, store, channel, and treat water at various stages of this cycle, all with the purpose of making water easily and cheaply available to citizens, agriculture, and industry. These innovations have helped civilizations across the world thrive and grow and are largely responsible for the world as we know it today.

However, we are realizing that smart water management requires understanding how "small water" works as part of a decentralized architecture, on a more personal basis, and not as a perpetual gift from nature. I discovered that I had to think differently about big water, which many consider free and a natural right, and to start thinking more about small water as a valuable asset that needs to be protected, maintained, and used productively. I began developing a working thesis that although big water still needs to be invested in and managed, it is likely that the ultimate solution to our challenges in water will come from innovations in how we develop and adapt to small water.

The good news is that despite, and in many ways because of, the growing sense of crisis about water, there are a wide variety of exciting opportunities for change driven by technology, management practices, government policy, and public perception that will help relieve and resolve the crisis over time. As is usual with major crises, the beneficial changes will be delayed by the inertia that comes from decades and centuries of practice and behavior that are rapidly becoming obsolete. However, for a variety of economic and marketing reasons, the corporate world is stepping in to take on the challenges of water sustainability and to demonstrate some of the upside potential for water sustainability.

THE WATER TRIP

My deep interest in water sustainability was stimulated by a 2010 spring break trip during my second year at the Stanford Graduate School of Business. The journey started when my friend Tom Mercer pitched an idea to me: we should partner up and lead a spring break road trip with a theme of water as a resource in the American Southwest. Unlike typical spring break trips, we would first convince our school administration to fund us, spend considerable time planning the journey, and convince a group of our peers to join us. Our efforts would culminate in a trek up and down the West Coast in a minivan to see what truth we could find in water.

Although I had my doubts that we could successfully convince a critical mass of fifteen other business school students to spend their spring break geeking out on water instead of jetting to an exotic locale, I said yes. I said yes because I felt irresponsible as a person devoting her career to shifting the world toward a more sustainable future while not understanding how water really works. I had faith that this trip would be the perfect crash course.

So we enlisted our friend Lazeena Rahman to join the planning team and quickly set to work unraveling the tangled, knotted mess that is water in the American Southwest. We initiated the process with a required reading list: Marc Reisner's book *Cadillac Desert: The American West and Its Disappearing Water,* the quintessential historical tome on the cowboy development of water west of 104°

longitude, along with the global water reports from McKinsey & Company, the World Economic Forum, the Environmental Defense Fund, and the World Wildlife Federation. We tacked on a few lyrical and romantic accounts of water from local poets and a short essay by Joan Didion. And of course we made time for a viewing of the classic movie *Chinatown*, with its film noir treatment of the California water wars of the 1920s.[1]

Once I read the water reports, it was easy to see that the term "water" actually means different things to different people, most of whom rarely reach consensus on anything. I also realized that the water debate was at the same stage that the debate on clean energy had been about ten years earlier. The documents highlighted the battles over the pricing of water, the irrigation practices in the Central and Imperial Valleys of California, the demand for energy to move water all around the state to places it does not naturally want to go, and the techniques of the basic delivery of clean water to individual households.

After fifteen months of research, reading, discovery, investigation, outreach, and grunt work, we were ready for our trip. The final itinerary was designed to follow the flow of water through the state. We kicked off the trip with a few infrastructure tours around the San Joaquin River delta. We then stopped in the capital city of Sacramento for some time with government officials, farm-hopped through the east side of the Central Valley, bounced around Los An-

---

1 Marc Reisner, *Cadillac Desert: The American West and Its Disappearing Water* (New York: Viking Press, 1986); McKinsey & Company, "Charting Our Water Future: Economic Frameworks to Inform Decision-Making," 2009; World Economic Forum, "Innovative Water Partnerships: Experiences, Lessons Learned, and Proposed Way Forward," 2010, www.weforum.org/issues/water; Spreck Rosekrans and Ann H. Hayden, "Finding the Water," Environmental Defense Fund, 2005; World Wildlife Federation, "Rich Countries, Poor Water," 2006; Joan Didion, "Holy Water," in *The White Album* (New York: Farrar, Straus & Giroux, 1990); *Chinatown*, directed by Roman Polanski, Paramount Pictures, 1974.

geles and Orange County, and then took a big left turn to the city in the desert, Las Vegas. Our trip ended in style with a visit to the mighty Hoover Dam.

Before departing on our journey, we had assumed not only that we would be directly exposed to the problems of water management but also that as enterprising, problem-solving, MBA candidates, we would discover the solutions to fix those problems, or at least to capitalize on them.

But the reality was quite different. We found a jumble of conflicting technologies, infrastructure approaches, and policies. We saw one instance after another of man versus nature, man's control of nature, and nature's slap in the face in response to human domination. We interacted with people and saw how water impacts everyone in so many ways. Alas, we were not able to find the solutions to today's water dilemmas, but we saw and learned much more than we expected.

Our first big discovery about the conflict of policy, environment, and technology took place on the first day of our journey at the Tracy Fish Facility at the mouth of the Delta-Mendota Canal, which is part of the Central Valley Project system of aqueducts. The center was built in part to preserve the delta smelt, a small fish officially protected by the Endangered Species Act. Although this facility is small, it is quite significant because it influences the amount of water released down the aqueducts to Central Valley.

The main attraction was the large fish rack wedged into the mouth of the canal. The way it works is simple. The rack first traps the small fish attempting to swim down the aqueduct and then funnels them through pipes into a big tank. A state employee periodically scoops some fish from the tank to sample and identify which species failed at their escape plan. If he finds a delta smelt, he must then follow a protocol by chopping off its head, bagging it, tagging it, and shipping it off to a research laboratory. The other fish swimming in the tank are then transferred via a water tank truck that drives one hundred miles back up Interstate 5 to dump them back into the delta.

Although this process was likely based on good and logical intentions, we found it astonishing that the facility built to ensure the protection of a certain species of fish was actually decapitating the endangered little guys and sending the other innocent species off to get snacked on by the other predatory delta fish who likely had figured out the routine.

Another very surprising moment of the trip was when we visited a small farming village a few miles outside of Visalia in the heart of California's Central Valley. It was a gorgeous, sunny day in the village surrounded by citrus groves. The community was composed of farmworker families who earn their livelihoods by irrigating, fertilizing, and harvesting the fruits, nuts, and vegetables in the region, which supplies a significant amount of food to the United States and abroad. The dramatic backdrop of the village was the mighty Sierra Nevada range, cutting a jagged line into the sky and capped with the fresh, clean snow that melts and runs down the slopes into streams and rivers to supply much of the state's freshwater.

We were given a tour by a longtime Visalia resident who described the local issues with contaminated groundwater. Over time the fertilizer runoff from the surrounding farms had leached into the groundwater supply, contaminating it with deadly nitrates that were harming the health of the community members. As a result, state health officials instructed the community to not drink the water the town supplied. Instead they were encouraged to buy expensive bottled water for their daily needs on top of their monthly bills to the water utility. Efforts had been made by members of the community to encourage the farms in the area to change their irrigation and fertilization practices. Yet because the farms also employed most of the working people in the community, the intensity of the change efforts was muted by the fear of evaporating employment. As we spoke, the striking beauty of the backdrop of the Sierra snowpack in spring, the surrounding lush orchards, and the green lawns masked the public health danger hidden in the invisible poisonous water table underneath our feet.

Our last stop took us to a striking piece of infrastructure, the Hoover Dam. As a trained civil engineer, I do get excited about massive man-made structures, and Hoover Dam is a thing of beauty—a visual masterpiece that balances human ingenuity with the earth's powerful forces. It tamed a mighty river but looks like classic art deco. This artistic, concrete fortress of a dam uses the forces of the geological formation around it to harness the potential energy of the Colorado River watershed. The adjacent museums help remind us of the people and community that came together to make it happen. The project was an unprecedented accomplishment at a significant point in history, completed in 1936 through the efforts of thousands of workers in the midst of the world's greatest economic depression.

Our group was lucky enough to receive a special tour from one of the chief engineers, so we walked through the deep tunnels behind the dam, saw the powerful turbines that convert the water's energy into electricity, and met the people who make the place work. A couple of the turbines were actually out of operation because they were being upgraded to improve their performance. By replacing a few parts, the engineers could shave off a couple minutes from the time it took to start the turbines spinning, from zero to full operation. This would allow Hoover Dam's energy generation capacity to become more valuable in producing variable power, which could improve electrical grid condition, especially as the grid had more decentralized renewable sources come online. Those two minutes could make a dramatic difference.

The tour ended on an incongruous note when our guide revealed to us that the dam was facing a new kind of problem: a nonindigenous species of tiny quagga mussels was invading Lake Mead. These pesky little crustaceans, smaller than our palms, were proliferating at an unmanageable pace and had an affinity for the nearby metal and steel infrastructure. The turbines couldn't function properly if too many mussels muscled their way in. Frustrated engineers are still looking for the remedy.

The visit revealed the striking realities challenging the Hoover Dam: the plummeting level of Lake Mead, the silting up of the reservoir, and the downstream and upstream changes to the hydrodynamics and biodiversity of the Colorado River. It also showed us how big water can change, for good and ill, the economic and natural state of an entire region.

These anecdotes illustrate how so many worlds collide around the resource of water. And although our busload of water enthusiasts ended the trip exhausted and confused, we were all hooked by the challenges we'd glimpsed. We had seen firsthand a hodgepodge of a system that was the legacy of adventurers, explorers, local and state governments, industry, agriculture, suburban sprawl, environmental enthusiasts, and even nonhuman species. This system, which in many ways celebrates the intellectual and physical accomplishments of humanity, also demonstrates the long-run fragility of this system, and why we need to improve and innovate around how these systems are created and managed in the future.

WATER AND THE WORLD ECONOMY

I wish I could replicate this road trip at one hundred different locations around the world. The water resource challenge is often regional in nature, so the details are nuanced and varied. But when you think about water from the industrial and corporate point of view, it is a bit easier from a macro and even global perspective to measure and focus on the problems and the potential solutions.

Water is not just for drinking and bathing. Every product we buy, every meal we eat, and every service we receive involves the use of water. Parts manufacturing companies need water to cool the machines that make things. Data centers that run the Internet cloud on which we now store the data of our lives need water to cool their millions of computer servers. Food companies and farmers need water to grow and package food and biofuels. The entertainment and tourism industries need water to provide activities that are fun and recreational. The energy industry needs water both to extract fuel from the earth and to cool the generation equipment that consumes the fuel to produce power. And in the case of hydroelectricity, water itself is the fuel.

So whether you work for IBM, Google, Del Monte, or the Professional Golfers Association, water is one of the most important resources on which your business depends. A minor change, such as a shortage of industrial water supply or a small increase in the price of water, could cause dramatic ripple effects throughout the economy. Water instantly transforms into a global management consideration once the conventional perception of cheap and abundant water shifts toward a reality where water is precious and highly valuable.

Of course, an economic commodity like water cannot be managed unless its impact can be measured. And just as we can measure the carbon footprint of each product or service we consume (that is, the amount of carbon dioxide waste produced in the creation or delivery of that product or service), we can also measure its water footprint (the amount of water consumed or used to create the product or service).

Another way to measure water's impact on the economy is to consider the importance of "solid-water products," that is, products that have water as a large percentage of their content or that require large amounts of water, relative to other resources, for their production. Although there are a variety of finished goods that could be put into this category, including pharmaceuticals, building materials, and clothing, foodstuffs might be the best example. In geopolitical terms, countries that have plentiful water tend to be net exporters of food, whereas countries that have a scarcity of water tend to be net importers. Over time the cost of labor will become less important to producing food than the cost of water. Thus, water is becoming as important in global trade balances as it is in domestic economies. Already we are seeing global economic entities such as General Electric, Procter & Gamble, Cargill, China Development Bank, and McDonald's buying controlling interests in companies and organizations that have assets in food-exporting (that is, solid water–exporting) countries such as Brazil, Canada, and Australia.

WATER SUSTAINABILITY— A NEW SOURCE OF ECONOMIC ADVANTAGE

Water, then, is at the heart of the global economy. This creates obvious risks for all of us, including business leaders. But it also creates enormous emerging opportunities.

The past one hundred years of the practice and science of management have resulted in major increases in labor productivity through the growing use of tools, machinery, computers, and automation. This labor productivity improvement has resulted in major increases in wealth and the quality of life for the portions of the world that have been able to deploy these assets.

By contrast, water productivity has increased only modestly over the past century. Water productivity relates to how much economic value is created by one unit of water or how much water is required to deliver one unit of a product or service. Improving water productivity means that businesses use less water to produce more economic items, such as grains, meat, clothing, electronics, and automobiles. Improving water productivity means that consumers use less water in their everyday lives with the same or better quality of life. Making our businesses and industries water-sustainable means they have managed to improve their water productivity to the point that their demand is equal to or less than the supply. Although improvement in water productivity has been modest, the good news is that there is much room for further improvement and a host of emerging tools to help make it happen.

As the price of water increases and its availability decreases, each industry and business that depends on this resource will have to plan and innovate accordingly. Just as the cost of labor drives industries to invest in capital equipment and automation to improve productivity or move from a high-labor-cost country to a lower-labor-cost country, the cost of water will create similar challenges for business.

There are several examples today of companies that are making major changes in their approach to business to improve their water productivity and therefore are being proactive in growing their competitive advantage. Some are driven by the marketing benefits that come from being identified as a sustainable or water-conscious company. Some are driven by wanting to be a leader in sustainability and satisfying an emerging market segment. And many are just applying smart management principles by designing their business operations to trim wasteful practices and operate in a lean manner.

When I think about small water in the context of the messy ecosystem of the corporate world, I mentally sort companies into three categories: existing companies that have water as their core business; existing companies that don't have water as their core business; and new ventures that are innovating in water. Each category can find ways to innovate around water to create competitive advantages.

The core water companies include a broad range of firms, such as local, urban, and regional water utilities, bottled water companies, large agriculture firms, food processors, biofuel energy companies, sewage treatment plants, desalination facilities, and hydroelectric companies. A continual focus on water as a resource is obvious for these firms.

Non-core water companies include just about every other mature company. Most companies in this category are just beginning to analyze and understand how their use of water offers room to improve efficiency, new business opportunities to be pursued through innovation, or new marketing opportunities to communicate the quality or value of their products versus their competition. For a growing number of these firms, the resource of water is becoming a more important factor in the planning and execution of business strategies.

The fashion and textile worlds have been two of the first to jump on the water minibus. For example, in 2011 Levi's introduced an entirely new line of products called Water<Less jeans. The name is derived from the fact that, although the average pair of jeans uses forty-two liters of water in the finishing process, the Water<Less collection reduces water consumption by an average of 28 percent. Perhaps there are product designers at Levi's or at their competitors thinking about how to design new products that require no water at all in the finishing process. Certainly the design for sustainability community would advocate such an approach.

In the construction industry, green building and other sustainability standards, including the well-known LEED, already have helped encourage the implementation of new best practices for water efficiency, sustainability, and marketing benefits. The Solaire building in New York City's Battery Park includes a water recycling system in addition to solar power and other green technologies, which earned the building a gold certification from LEED. The Cool Roof Rating Council was created solely to provide a mechanism by which companies that make roofing materials could have a way to measure and communicate to the market how innovative they have been in making their products contribute to sustainable buildings. The water connection? Cooler roofs mean less air conditioning, which means less water used for climate control.

Even renewable energy companies that are not based on hydro-power are starting to understand how their water footprint can become a valuable competitive asset. The company I work for, Vestas Wind Systems, the world's largest wind energy equipment company, has begun to design its market communications and service offerings around the fact that its water footprint is zero, since no water is used or consumed when wind energy generates electricity. This focus is especially important for electrifying parts of the world that are short on water and heavy on wind, particularly in desert regions. Vestas technology improves overall project economics and increases the number of global sites where wind energy would be attractive. By using water as an economic guide, it can actually help identify and evaluate the most attractive wind-power markets while at the same time contributing to improve practical water sustainability in those areas.

Many long-established technology firms are starting to realize that their expertise can be applied in tangible and meaningful approaches in the water market. IBM is applying its expertise through the company's Smarter Planet initiative with the goal of establishing a market-leading position in the groundwater monitoring market. Right now very few businesses know how many gallons of water they are pumping out of the ground for consumption. Imagine a building with no gas or electric meters, and think about the waste this would promote; water is currently managed in just such a dysfunctional fashion. As a global leader in monitoring and computation, IBM is actively carving out an early position in the potentially significant new market for water-use monitoring and control equipment—a smart way to realize financial benefits from the growing pressure on businesses to achieve water sustainability.

Perhaps most exciting is the third category of companies—ambitious start-ups that are innovating around water, hoping to improve the world while making money doing it. I have seen demonstrations of remarkable new products and services ranging from water sprinklers that use satellite communication to get weather forecasts for smart irrigation to technologies that combine physical sensors and the knowledge of plant biology to determine how much water grapevines need in a vineyard. More people are starting to look into how to grow more food with less water and how to capture and store water effectively so that previously fallow land becomes attractive for agriculture. Urban farming companies are sprouting up in cities across America, offering new solutions for urban runoff and local food supply challenges. Today's water nerds now have a chance to capitalize on their vast knowledge and maybe become as cool—and as wealthy—as the computer nerds.

Although water innovation ventures are still a small part of the entire clean-tech arena, investment opportunities in water technology are growing. Every venture capitalist I have talked with over the past year has told me he or she is extremely interested in investing in water innovation, although many are not sure where to look. The typical venture investment model requires a significant financial return in five to seven years, which is a very short time frame given the history of the water industry and the relatively low market price of water in most parts of the world. However, as the world water crisis intensifies, the investment dynamics will change. Investment levels for water innovation businesses from the venture industry currently measure over $100 million per year. At the same time, significant investment is going into new water innovation products and services from companies such as GE, Siemens, Grundfos, Danfoss, and IBM.

FUTURE OPPORTUNITIES FROM WATER SUSTAINABILITY INNOVATION

Many innovations and trends, mostly in the small water category, will drive future improvements in water productivity and enable more and more organizations to realize a competitive advantage based on their sustainable use of water. Five categories of trends are particularly notable.

Water conservation—changing the way corporations decide to use water. There are many corporate equivalents to the wasting of water by individual consumers by taking long showers or running the faucet while brushing teeth; in fact, it has been estimated that over 50 percent of water consumption in the United States could be eliminated with conservation. Many corporations have yet to even inventory all of the potential opportunities for improvement in the reduction of water, but others, in industries ranging from apparel and golfing to data center management, are getting more serious about identifying, measuring, and reducing their water use with pragmatic changes in practices and technology.

Changes in regulatory policy and utility pricing mechanisms could help strengthen and expand this trend. Utility customers in communities ranging from New York City to Palo Alto, California, have recently experienced net monthly billing increases after reducing their water consumption at the request of the utilities; it seems that the conservation worked, there was less demand for water, and the fixed costs of the utilities had to be spread across fewer gallons of water delivered. Such pricing policies create perverse incentives by "punishing" companies that are better at conserving water; they need to be changed.

Decentralized water grids for smaller entities. A number of new products and services will come to market over the next few years that will make it feasible for corporate and community planners to start designing water delivery grids at the scale of neighborhoods, homes, farms, business parks, corporate facilities, schools, and parks. At these scales, equipment and infrastructure can be implemented for water capture, storage, reuse, and purification. Again, implementing these solutions is easier said than done; it will require changes in local, state, regional, and federal regulations that today favor large centralized utilities. This approach will also require investment by government and industry in the commercial innovation of the necessary small or decentralized water grid technology. This may require a deregulation of the water industry to eliminate the barriers and disincentives created by the utility monopolies. It is a complex world that is full of opportunity for all players.

Water recycling and reuse. The opportunity for significant reductions in water consumption will continue to grow as innovative new products to facilitate cost-effective water purification and recycling come to market. Several industries, such as golf courses and sporting venues, have implemented extensive water recycling systems. However, the concept of recycling water to reuse it on a very local scale faces barriers in the form of public opinion and public health officials who have been trained to think only of big water. Hopefully, as more information and more effective products become available, these obstacles will begin to fall.

Local water harvesting. Big water harvesting can be seen in the man-made lakes and reservoirs built over the past one hundred years. However, if the concept and reality of decentralized water grids become possible and the recycling and reuse of water becomes a reality, then localized water harvesting will be an easy transition. And as we increase the productivity of the water we use, we will need to harvest less of it.

Smart water grid. This includes building intelligent measurement and management systems into appliances that use water as well as water meters. There is a huge market opportunity here for industries that help make antiquated processes smarter.

Although the changes necessary to realize many of the opportunities listed above will require big decisions on the state, regional, and national levels, businesses and industries are making many decisions now to implement small-water solutions. They are using economic analysis tools that include the cost to their businesses of the full economic value of water they use and are taking the risk to innovate with small-water technologies.

RECOGNIZING WATER SUSTAINABILITY AS A BUSINESS OPPORTUNITY

The growing corporate focus on water sustainability and productivity is much more than a fad. Remember that water has played a major role in the history of the global economy. The physical, political, and economic water systems that my friends and I visited during our California road trip are a legacy from a time when men and women were inspired by an optimistic vision of wealth generated through raw massive effort and unfettered ingenuity. Entrepreneurs from over a century ago were looking to make their fortune by managing and owning big water because it was the obvious precious resource that converted barren, dry land into a productive platform for farms, industry, and community. The business leaders of today are looking at small water as a key resource that they need to manage more effectively in their local and global supply chains. Of course, the pace of the change coming from this learning needs to accelerate, and being part of the catalytic process that is helping speed this change is one of the sources of my excitement and focus on water sustainability.

The concept of small water as a key economic resource and a new opportunity for market differentiation deserves a more prominent place in the thinking of today's business leaders. Fortunately, there is a growing global community of water experts who are working hard to assemble the data for business and engineering professions to use as they begin to recognize the value of water, realize that

this value will be essential in competing globally, and start to innovate in how to use it efficiently and effectively. Now is the right time
for members of the business community, whether they help to run
large global firms, regional businesses, or small entrepreneurial ventures, to seize on the opportunities to make water economically ad-
vantageous while at the same time making it less scarce and a more
sustainable resource for everyone.

10

DIAMONDS IN DISGUISE

Using Price Signals and
Market Forces to Address the Water Crisis

Robert Glennon

Robert Glennon is the Morris K. Udall Professor of Law and Public Policy in the Rogers College of Law at the University of Arizona. He is the author of the highly acclaimed *Water Follies: Groundwater Pumping and the Fate of America's Fresh Waters* (Washington, DC: Island Press, 2002). His latest book, *Unquenchable: America's Water Crisis and What to Do About It,* was published in April 2009.

In 2010 the Society of Environmental Journalists bestowed on *Unquenchable* a Rachel Carson Book Award for Reporting on the Environment and *Trout* magazine gave it an Honorable Mention in its list of "must-have books" ever published on the environment.

Glennon has been a guest on *The Daily Show with Jon Stewart, Talk of the Nation* with Neal Conan, *The Diane Rehm Show,* C-SPAN2's *Book TV,* and numerous other television and radio shows. His writings have appeared in the *Washington Post,* the *Arizona Republic,* the *Boston Globe,* and the *Arizona Daily Star.* He occasionally blogs for the Huffington Post.

Glennon has been a consultant and adviser to government agencies, corporations, NGOs, and law firms. Since 2009 his speaking schedule has taken him to more than twenty-five states and to Switzerland, Canada, Singapore, Australia, and Saudi Arabia.

Glennon received a Juris Doctor from Boston College Law School and master's and doctoral degrees in American history from Brandeis University. He is a member of the bars of Arizona and Massachusetts.

In the United States, while we fret about running out of oil, we often overlook the fact that water lubricates our economy just as oil does—and water is in increasingly short supply. Evidence of the water crisis facing the United States is overwhelming: mandatory conservation programs, dried-up rivers and lakes, plummeting water tables, fallowed fields, canceled building projects, laid-off workers, polluted aquifers, desiccated wetlands, withered crops, shuttered factories, trucked-in water, canceled fishing seasons, collapsed pipes, subsided land, discolored tap water, closed power plants, increasing dust storms, dangerous wildfires, and persistent drought.

Yet despite these grave warning signals, the looming crisis remains largely invisible. We Americans are lucky: when we turn on our taps, we (usually) get a limitless quantity of safe drinking water for less than we pay for cell phone service or cable television. Most of us take this astonishing fact for granted. We think of water as we do the air, as infinite and inexhaustible.

Of course, this isn't true. Industrial and agricultural pollution has rendered many aquifers unfit for human use. Diversions from rivers have reduced flows in countless rivers and completely dried up others. And excessive groundwater pumping has lowered the water table in aquifers around the United States. It took thousands of years for this underground supply to accumulate, but we've depleted much of it in mere decades. Add in the stresses of global climate change, population growth, and internal migration (from humid regions to arid ones), and the reality is that we're using water in an unsustainable fashion.

We have options to keep the crisis from becoming a catastrophe, including conservation programs, reuse of reclaimed water, and desalination of ocean or brackish water. But these options, even in combination, will not end the crisis. We must do more. And one of the most important strategies we should employ is the use of price signals to encourage conservation and market incentives to encourage the reallocation of water from lower-value to higher-value uses.

THE DIAMOND-WATER PARADOX

In his groundbreaking 1776 treatise, *The Wealth of Nations,* economist Adam Smith described "the diamond-water paradox." Diamonds are incredibly expensive even though, as jewels, they have no utilitarian value. On the other hand, water, which is not only useful but also essential to life, is incredibly cheap. As Smith explained, the basic law of supply and demand explains this phenomenon: the price of an object goes up or down in response to its availability. Diamonds are scarce, and therefore costly; water is plentiful, and therefore cheap.

A more sophisticated explanation of the paradox focuses on the concept of marginal utility. If we were to ask a man dying of thirst in a desert how much he would pay for a diamond as compared to a gallon of water, we would find that the water is more valuable to him. But today, despite the potentially dramatic increase in the marginal utility of water as droughts and shortages worsen, we continue to squander this precious resource.

Think of our water supply as a giant milk-shake glass, and think of each user as putting a straw in the glass. Most states in the United States allow anyone to put a new straw in the glass. In Georgia, for example, there is no need to even get a permit to drill a groundwater well unless you're going to pump more than 100,000 gallons of water per day. That's more than 36 million gallons per year for each and every well, all of it completely unregulated.

We can't manage what we don't measure. Water is a critical public resource that all levels of government should protect—but we simply don't do it.

Some communities, such as Fresno, California, have resisted installing water meters in homes, which means residents' use is unmeasured. Fresno charges residents an archaic flat rate regardless of how much water they use. This pricing system encourages profligate water use, hovering around 300 gallons per person per day in

Fresno, while residents of neighboring Clovis, which has meters, use about 200 gallons each. Flat rates encourage waste and punish those who conserve.[1]

Is Fresno an anomaly? Unfortunately, it has lots of company: one-third of water utilities in the United States use flat-fee rates.

Similarly unmetered are wells in California's vast Central Valley, where farmers rely largely on groundwater to irrigate their fields. No one knows precisely how much water they pump. And farmers pay nothing to tap into this public supply.

Farmers aren't alone in getting free water. In cities across the United States, the water bills customers pay to municipal water departments or to private utilities are based on a cost-of-service principle. Water rates are set to generate a revenue stream equal to the cost of providing the service. Customers are paying for the extraction, storage, delivery, and treatment of water, but not for the water itself. The water is free.

And exactly how low are our water bills? According to one 2011 survey, Americans pay an average of $10.19 for 1,000 gallons of municipal water and sewer service. That's about a penny per gallon. A typical family spends $523 per year on water and wastewater. That's less than the $707 they spend on soft drinks and bottled water. It's about one-half of what Northern Europeans spend for water service, and less than any other developed country, except Canada.[2]

Rates vary substantially across the country, with residents of rain-blessed cities, such as Seattle, Boston, and Atlanta, paying *more* than arid southwestern cities, such as Las Vegas, Los Angeles, and

---

1 Robert Glennon, *Unquenchable: America's Water Crisis and What to Do About It* (Washington, DC: Island Press, 2009), 222–223.

2 U.S. Environmental Protection Agency, "Water & Wastewater Pricing—Introduction," http://water.epa.gov/infrastructure/sustain/Water-and-Wastewater-Pricing-Introduction .cfm; and Glennon, *Unquenchable*, 223–224.

Phoenix. This paradoxical disparity is due to the recent surge in wastewater rates as older cities with decaying infrastructure upgrade their treatment facilities. Sometimes they do so voluntarily; often it's to settle litigation brought by the US Environmental Protection Agency (EPA) to enforce the Clean Water Act.

As cheap as municipal rates are, farmers get an even better deal. Agricultural rates for water use are low in part because it's unnecessary to treat irrigation water to drinking-water standards. Another reason is that farmers in the West receive heavily subsidized water. In the Imperial Irrigation District in Southern California, farmers pay one penny for approximately 216 gallons of water. (Remember, municipal rates are about a penny per gallon.) But if you think *this* must the best deal ever, you're wrong. A few years ago in Nebraska, a water provider raised its rates so that farmers had to pay one penny for 1,080 gallons—and the decision evoked controversy. When the price paid for water is staggeringly low, farmers have little incentive to conserve.

PROBLEMS WITH CHEAP/FREE WATER

Such low rates for water create several problems as we struggle with water scarcity. First, as we've already seen, they encourage waste and discourage conservation. Second, low rates do not account for the real cost of water. Economists agree that the real cost of water is its *replacement* cost—that is, the marginal cost for a water provider to obtain additional supplies of water. Instead most utilities charge far less, subsidizing current uses by encouraging unsustainable use of water.

Third, low rates fail to include adequate funds to maintain, repair, and replace the nation's aging water and wastewater infrastructure. Alas, the nation's 1.5 million miles of water and wastewater

pipes, 54,000 drinking-water systems, and 17,000 wastewater treatment plants are in desperate need of upgrading. This failure to maintain properly our water and wastewater systems should not come as
a surprise given recent economic conditions and political reality.
Anti-tax, anti-government-spending fervor is higher today than ever
before, and maintaining infrastructure isn't the kind of showy program voters are willing to support. No politician is eager to run for
reelection on the campaign slogan, "I overhauled the sewer system."

But deferred maintenance carries a heavy price, beginning with
frequent pipe bursts and sewer overflows. In Philadelphia, for example, where some of the city's pipes are almost two hundred years
old, roughly eight hundred ruptures in water and sewer lines occur
annually. Nationwide, the EPA estimates that 240,000 water-main
breaks occur each year, wasting water directly, squandering billions
of dollars spent to treat water, and causing outbreaks of disease from
sewage overflows.[3]

Still, raising water rates poses dicey problems for politicians.
Nothing boils the blood of voters quicker than a proposal to increase
their water bills. Local newspapers fuel the flames: headlines may
warn of a proposed 19 percent increase, which sounds shocking, because a small increase to a low monthly bill yields a high percentage
hike. Few voters do the math and recognize that a 19 percent increase
might cost consumers only 21 cents per day. City council meetings
often turn contentious over proposed hikes that would add less to a
household's monthly bill than the cost of a single Starbucks latte.

Rather than risk annoying voters, politicians instead instruct
their water departments to develop conservation plans to handle
water shortages. Some of these plans tap into community goodwill

---

3 Brett Walton, "The Price of Water: A Comparison of Water Rates, Usage in 30 US Cities,"
Circle of Blue, April 26, 2010, www.circleofblue.org/waternews/2010/world/the
-price-of-water-a-comparison-of-water-rates-usage-in-30-u-s-cities.

with pleas for citizens to reduce water use voluntarily. Others involve mandatory restrictions on certain uses, such as watering lawns, filling swimming pools, or washing cars. Still others restrict water use during certain hours of the day or days of the week.

Some conservation programs work beautifully and help instill a community culture of conservation. Cities such as Long Beach, Albuquerque, San Antonio, and Tucson have pioneering conservation programs. But some programs can produce unintended consequences. Consider recent events in Los Angeles and Texas. In response to drought conditions in 2009, Los Angeles limited the use of lawn sprinklers to Mondays and Thursdays. The restrictions dramatically reduced water use. But the city simultaneously suffered a record number of water-main bursts. A blue-ribbon panel of scientists determined that pressure in the city's aging system of pipes dropped on the days watering was allowed but increased on the other days. When the pressure built up, it accelerated the metal fatigue of old and corroded pipes, resulting in burst pipes, flooded streets, and damaged property.

In 2011, in the midst of the driest spell in Texas's recorded history, hundreds of cities and towns slapped restrictions on outdoor water use. Residents responded and water use declined. But the utilities' revenue stream, which was predicated on delivering a certain volume of water, also declined. The next step for Texas politicians will be a tricky one. Having cajoled or ordered their constituents to conserve water, politicians must raise water rates to recapture the lost revenue: "Thanks for being good citizens; here's your reward!" If Texas utilities had increased water prices during the drought, they could have maintained their revenue stream yet succeeded in conserving water. And they would have avoided the costs associated with monitoring and enforcing prohibitions on outdoor uses. But our dominant cultural assumption—that the price of water should remain ultracheap—stood in the way.

WHAT SHOULD WE DO?

If we in the United States are to maintain our proud tradition of universal access to safe drinking water, we must be good stewards of this precious resource. And that moral obligation carries with it an obligation to put our money where our values are—which means paying the *true* value of the water we use.

Yet raising water rates poses its own moral challenge, because water is, after all, essential for life. How do we protect people of modest income to ensure they have the water they need? Peter Gleick and his colleagues at the Pacific Institute have calculated how much water each person needs daily for drinking, cooking, bathing, and sanitation: about thirteen gallons. The total is less than 1 percent of the water used in the United States every day.

We should recognize a human right to water for these essential purposes. If the richest country in the history of the world can't make that commitment to its people, then we're a sorry lot. But water use beyond this threshold often involves discretionary uses, such as filling swimming pools or watering lush landscapes. Water rates should target such uses to encourage conservation. If people want to water shrubs and lawns or fill pools, they can still do so— but they should pay the real cost for these personal choices.

Increasing water rates will have several benefits. It will encourage all users to consider the financial consequences of how they use water and for what purpose. Current rate structures in many cities send exactly the opposite signal. One-third of American municipalities utilize a decreasing block rate structure. In other words, the more water you use, the cheaper the last unit of water is, which encourages waste. We need to reverse that incentive by using tiered rates that increase at specified volumes.

Perhaps the most critical benefit of pricing water appropriately would be to stimulate the use of new water-saving technologies. As I've traveled around the country talking about my book *Un-*

quenchable, I've regularly met inventors and engineers who have designed and created conservation products: water filters, low-flow devices, energy-saving delivery systems, desalination technologies, and reclaimed-water systems. Many of these technologies and inventions work! There is only one problem, and it's a big one. Few of these inventors and engineers have viable business models for marketing their products because the price of water is so low. Most citizens aren't willing to spend hundreds of dollars to save tens of dollars. And who can blame them?

Despite the impending water crisis, we continue to price water as though it were plentiful. Local governments are failing their stewardship responsibilities by allowing limitless access to a finite resource. Our moral obligation as stewards of the essence of life requires that we invert the diamond-water paradox. The first thirteen gallons per person per day should be free, but thousands of gallons to fill swimming pools should be expensive. Our obligation to future generations demands no less. As a Native American proverb instructs, "We do not inherit the earth, we borrow it from our children."

USING MARKET FORCES TO REALLOCATE WATER

Another way to halt the relentless, unsustainable use of water is to eliminate the luxury of letting anyone and everyone put new straws into the milk-shake glass. If someone wants to place a new demand on the public supply—insert a new straw—we should insist that he offset his new demand by persuading an existing user to remove her straw. A demand-offset system would encourage voluntary water transfers that would reallocate water from low-value uses to higher-value ones. By tapping into the power of markets, we can protect our environment, halt the overpumping of our aquifers, avoid the construction of costly and environmentally destructive dams and reservoirs, and improve the efficiency of our water use. Markets can also free up water for homegrown, job-generating companies, such as Google and Intel, which require large quantities of water to run their server farms and fabricate semiconductors.

In Santa Fe, New Mexico, the city council responded to a 2002 drought by requiring all new construction to offset the water that the development would use. For example, developers could obtain a permit to build if they retrofitted existing homes with low-flow toilets. This system did not halt development; it required developers to underwrite new water conservation measures.

Most developers actually liked this system, especially compared with its alternative: a ban on new construction. And Santa Fe plumbers jumped at the opportunity for new business. Existing residents welcomed the chance to get free toilets. Within a couple of years, plumbers had swapped out most of the old water-wasting toilets with new high-efficiency ones. Water that residents would needlessly have flushed away was now being used to supply new homes.

Building on this successful program, in 2005 the Santa Fe city council began to require developers to tender water rights to the city with their building permit applications. In short order, a market emerged as developers began to buy water rights from farmers, who had been using the water to grow low-value crops, such as alfalfa. Developers deposited the water rights in a water bank, much like the rest of us would deposit a check. When the development became shovel-ready, the developer withdrew the water for the project; if her project stalled, she sold the rights to another developer whose project was further along. Thanks to these innovative measures, along with an aggressive water conservation program and increasing block rates, water use per person in Santa Fe has dropped 42 percent since 1995.[4]

Santa Fe's water rights transfer process can serve as a model for the rest of the country. It links land use decisions to the city's available

---

4 Ibid.

water supply. Construction can occur only if there is water to support it. The costs of acquiring new water for growth are absorbed by those who would like to insert a new straw into the milk-shake glass.

Given the extent of the water crisis in the United States, innovation in cities alone will not meet increasing demands. We should encourage agricultural producers to innovate as well. Irrigating crops is very water-intensive. Nationwide, farmers consume between 70 percent and 80 percent of our water. Traditional irrigation methods involve crudely dug ditches that divert water from rivers, and canal gates that open to flood the fields. A large percentage of the water that farmers withdraw from rivers never reaches the fields; instead it percolates into the ground. Flood irrigation, the least efficient method, results in additional losses due to evaporation and runoff, but it's used on almost half of the 60 million irrigated acres in the United States. The most efficient method—micro-irrigation, which emits a precise quantity of water to each plant or tree—is used on only 6 percent. So there is tremendous room for improvement, but the shift to more efficient methods is occurring very slowly.

History explains this troubling reality. Farmers began irrigating in the nineteenth century under a legal doctrine known as prior appropriation. This traditional first-in-time is first-in-right rule protects the earliest diverters by recognizing a property right in the use of water. Water in the United States is a public resource owned by the state. But states have accorded rights to *use* the water to farmers, miners, cities, industries, and homeowners.

These "use rights" developed when water was plentiful and the government wanted to reward those intrepid souls who sought to eke out a living from irrigating crops. As a result, the legal system developed a curious notion of "wasting" water. If a farmer failed to divert his full entitlement of water, then he was wasting it (in other words, not using it beneficially). If a farmer didn't use all his water, then he risked losing his right to it under the doctrines of abandonment and forfeiture. To modern sensibilities, these legal rules seem bizarre: because water is scarce, we should encourage farmers to use less water rather than penalize them for doing so.

How, then, should we overhaul the nation's aged irrigation program? The government could simply order farmers to improve the efficiency of their delivery and irrigation systems, but most farmers run marginally profitable businesses. It could cost a farmer hundreds of thousands of dollars to line her ditches with concrete and to install micro-irrigation or center-pivot systems (the latter produce those huge green circles visible to airline passengers from 35,000 feet). Such a government mandate would impose enormous and unfair hardships on farmers, and given the power of the agricultural lobby, it's a political nonstarter.

Instead let's create an incentive for farmers to use less water. If farmers save water by using less or becoming more efficient, they should be allowed to sell or lease the water they conserve. Cities, businesses, miners, developers, or environmental organizations that need water can purchase the conserved water. This system places the financial burden of modernizing the nation's irrigation infrastructure on those who want to stick another straw in the glass. A regulated water market protects farmers and requires developers to foot the bill.

A vibrant water market has already emerged in the American West. An astonishing 10 trillion gallons—more than twice the annual flow of the Colorado River—was sold or leased in the twelve western states between 1987 and 2005. Many transfers were between farmers, to take advantage of commodity price shifts, but the bulk of the water was transferred from farmers to cities. That's the power of the marketplace allocating water where it's needed most rather than encouraging waste.[5]

---

5 Robert Glennon, Jedidiah Brewer, Alan Ker, and Gary Libecap, "Transferring Water in the American West: 1987–2005," *University of Michigan Journal of Law Reform* 40, no. 4 (Summer 2007): 1021–1053.

Two questions beg for answers: If farmers sell water, what will happen to the price of food? And what will happen to the farmers themselves? Observing what farmers have done answers both questions.

Farmers are savvy businesspeople who understand the opportunities markets provide. When a housing developer approaches a farmer with an offer to purchase some of her water rights, she has four options. First, she may decline, if the money isn't adequate or if she simply wants to continue using her entire allotment. Second, she can look around her farm and note that the forty acres behind the barn has mostly clay soil with a low crop yield of bushels per acre. She may decide to fallow this land and sell the conserved water to the developer.

Her third option is to use the proceeds from the sale to modernize her irrigation infrastructure. In the case of one rancher in Oregon, the $700,000 offered by the Oregon Water Trust allowed the family to install a center-pivot irrigation system, which was more efficient than the flood irrigation they traditionally used. The new system enabled them to grow just as much alfalfa but with less water—a win-win solution.

Finally, she may adjust her crop mix by entering higher-value niche markets, identifying new growing techniques, or moving to value-added products. One niche market, baby lettuces, has boomed in popularity over the past decade. Farmers who shift from iceberg lettuce to spring mixes generate higher revenues with lower labor costs and lower water consumption. In California's Coachella Valley, some farmers have switched from flood to drip irrigation and moved from growing alfalfa to growing higher-value dates, fruits, and vegetables. Their income rose as their water use dropped.

In many states farmers receive a modest income from irrigating crops that consume a large quantity of water. The best example is alfalfa, which is the fourth-largest crop in the United States. Produced in every state, alfalfa is grown on more than 23 million acres to feed farm animals, especially beef cattle and dairy herds. Alfalfa has attributes that make it a very attractive crop for farmers. It has high protein and low fiber; it's drought and salt tolerant; it grows well in poor soils with low-quality water. But when summer temperatures spike, alfalfa blooms quickly and deteriorates in quality. A diet of lower-grade alfalfa can reduce milk production by 50 percent and beef cattle weight gain from 1.85 pounds per day to 0.06 pounds.[6]

Low-quality alfalfa fetches next to nothing in the marketplace, yet farmers from Montana to California continue to grow it in scorching temperatures that range from the upper 90s to 115 degrees. They do so partly because they have always done so, partly because we have not given them an incentive to turn off their irrigation pumps during the dog days of summer. The enormous disparity in value between alfalfa and, say, the microprocessors that Intel Corporation could produce using the same water creates tremendous opportunities for trade in water rights. An acre-foot of water (approximately 325,000 gallons) used to grow alfalfa generates at most $264 for the farmer; that same amount of water used to manufacture Intel's Core 2 Duo chips generates $13 million.[7]

Let's return to our two questions about the effect of water markets on the price of food and on the farmers. The price of food *is* currently increasing, but not due to the cost of water. The spike in food prices comes from the rising costs of producing food, a disturbing decline in the number of acres of farmland lost to sprawling cities and endless suburbs, and competition with biofuel companies for corn used to refine ethanol. To satisfy new municipal, industrial, and environmental demands for water, we have already begun to

---

6 Glennon, *Unquenchable*, 273–274.

7 Ibid., 201.

reallocate water from low-value agricultural uses, including such nonfood crops as cotton. Reducing the amount of water used for crops, such as alfalfa and cotton, has not appreciably raised the price of food. United States consumers continue to enjoy the cheapest food on earth.

Nor has it adversely affected farmers. Even though farmers have sold trillions of gallons of water since 1985, aggregate farm revenue, held constant for inflation, has not declined. This startling conclusion confirms what we now know: farmers adjust to using less water by becoming more efficient. They fallow their least productive fields, modernize their irrigation system, or shift their crop mix.

The nation has a critical need to free up water for high-value uses, such as by manufacturers like Intel, by reallocating water from existing lower-value users. If we're not going to use voluntary, market-rooted transactions, there is really only one alternative: government mandates.

Throughout American history, government rules, regulations, and statutes have determined who gets to use water. The results of this political process should not comfort anyone. When elected officials or government agencies allocate water, their decisions inevitably favor the most powerful political and economic interests in the state. A market system of voluntary sales and leases offers an escape from a politically driven allocation system.

CHALLENGES IN DISRUPTING THE STATUS QUO

Markets, then, have many virtues. Mainstream economic theory maintains that markets make everyone better by encouraging innovation, promoting specialization, and moving goods to those who can make the best use of them. But markets do fail. Those who blindly worship at the altar of the free market tend to ignore the harsh consequences of unconstrained markets, including widespread unemployment, environmental degradation, and cultural destruction.

This realization is especially sobering in thinking about water. Critics of water marketing claim that it values water, a resource essential for life, as just another marketable commodity, no different than cell phones or video games. But in the United States, *water is already treated as an economic good,* though in an incomplete and disjointed manner. Ever since the 1850s, with the development of the prior appropriation system, states have recognized rights to use water. These use rights are property rights; in some states they're even conveyed by a deed, just as you would do for the sale of your home.

The right to water, then, is already treated as a commodity. Rather than decrying a system already in place, we should employ it to help us solve the water crisis. The absence of clear property rights in water is what got us into the crisis in the first place. By allowing limitless straws in the milk-shake glass, we encouraged grotesque overuse of the public resource. It's a classic example of what economists call the tragedy of the commons: because no one had exclusive rights to the resource, everyone had an incentive to exploit it. If we strengthen the use rights that farmers already have in water by permitting them to sell or lease their water, we create incentives for farmers to utilize the resource more productively.

Markets ultimately depend on the state recognizing property rights and enforcing contracts. Because the operation of markets depends on political decisions the state makes, the state is ultimately responsible for the consequences. In the case of a market in water, we're talking about a public resource with cultural, spiritual, religious, environmental, and economic value. The state should play a critical role in protecting these noneconomic values.

Market failure sometimes produces what economists call externalities, which occur when an actor does not absorb the costs of his actions but instead sloughs them off on third parties. For example, a farmer who sells water to a city and shuts down part of his operation may end up firing some workers. The lost wages of the farmworkers are the result of the sale but are not a cost the farmer usually pays. Similarly, if a farmer diverts the entire flow of a stream, the fish downstream will die. The farmer may not pay for this harm to a public resource. Markets have difficulty figuring out how to make the person who generates these externalities pay for them.

That's where the state must play a role. If we're going to have a market in a public resource, the state must regulate it. The rationale for state oversight is to protect third parties (farmworkers and others harmed by water transfers) and to safeguard the environment. Securing water for high-value urban projects should not come at the expense of rural communities or the environment.

One other nagging question needs an answer: Won't well-heeled private companies always outbid nonprofit environmental organizations for water?

The answer: not necessarily. We've recently seen environmental organizations outbid ranchers for US Forest Service grazing leases. Water trusts have purchased or leased water from ranchers in several western states, including Montana and Washington, to secure flows for critical reaches of rivers. Environmentally conscious landowners have partnered with the Nature Conservancy in hundreds of transactions that have protected sensitive streams and rivers. In short, environmental organizations are already competing successfully in the market for water.

In addition, for most sales or leases of water, it really doesn't matter whether an environmental group has deeper pockets than the developer. A simple reallocation from an agricultural to an urban use is unlikely to cause environmental harm; the farmer is *already* diverting the water from the river or pumping it from the aquifer. But if a transfer *would* harm the environment, environmental groups can oppose it during the government review process.

For the environmental community, there is a much more important reason to support water marketing. Quite simply, the alternatives are horrible. No one is so naive as to think that population growth and economic development will simply cease. But where will the water come from to support these inevitable trends? If it's not transferred from existing users, then it will come from diverting more surface water, building additional dams, or drilling more wells. Each of these "solutions" should cause a shudder down the spine of any person who cares a whit about the environment.

BREAKING THE CYCLE

Water poses a vexing riddle: because we can neither make water nor destroy it, our supply is fixed. So why is it exhaustible? Because water is a shared resource, used and reused, and some uses preclude future reuse. A milk-shake glass full of straws forebodes inevitable doom.

But there is no reason to despair. We have a menu of options that recognize water as a valuable, exhaustible public resource. Conservation, desalination, and reuse are partial solutions for some communities. We must do more. In the United States, we should employ price signals to encourage water conservation and market forces to stimulate the reallocation of water. Pricing water sensibly and imposing a demand-offset requirement on all new uses of water can break the relentless cycle of overuse. We simply can't afford new straws in the glass.

Before the crisis turns into a catastrophe, we must chart a new course that values water as critical to sustaining our environment, maintaining public health, and stimulating our economy. Our collective lives depend on developing a new appreciation for water. Proven market systems and legal protocols can go a long way toward protecting water from heedless overuse. All we need now is the moral courage and political will to act.

11

TEN SIMPLE WAYS
YOU CAN HELP
PROTECT OUR WATER

The National Resources Defense Council

The Natural Resources Defense Council (NRDC) works to protect wildlife and wild places and to ensure a healthy environment for all life on Earth. Founded in 1970, NRDC harnesses the grassroots power of 1.3 million members and online activists with the courtroom clout and expertise of more than 350 lawyers, scientists, and other professionals. The NRDC Water Program works to ensure safe and sufficient water for people and the environment.

Water is fast becoming one of the most pressing environmental challenges of our time. Swelling demand is depleting aquifers and rivers; pollution from traditional and new sources is diminishing the utility of water to people and the environment; and climate change is exacerbating these challenges by altering rain- and snowfall patterns. There are a lot of red lights flashing on the dashboard.

The good news is that we know how to solve the water problems facing the nation. But we need to take action now. NRDC helped create the bedrock laws that safeguard our water—including the Clean Water Act—and we are designing solutions for the next generation of challenges. Today we are taking an integrated approach because the availability and quality of water are inextricably connected, and we recognize we can't solve one issue without solving the other.

And so green infrastructure—things such as pocket parks, green roofs, and permeable pavement—not only help recharge our ground-water supplies, but also keep dirty runoff away from our beaches. More efficient use of water in our communities—NRDC is helping create incentives so that all new homes built by 2025 use 25 percent less water—helps us preserve freshwater supplies and prepare for a changing climate at the same time.

NRDC is advocating forward-looking water solutions in the pol-icy arena, but individuals can make meaningful contributions in their everyday lives as well. What can you do right now? Here are ten simple steps you can take to help solve the water crisis.

IN YOUR HOME

- Correctly dispose of hazardous household products. Keep paints, used oil, cleaning solvents, pool chemicals, insecti-cides, and other hazardous household chemicals out of drains—and never pour them in storm sewers, where they can end up in nearby rivers and beaches.
- To avoid contaminating local waterways, choose nontoxic alternatives to household cleaners with harsh chemicals. You can use baking soda, for example, to deodorize drains, clean countertops, and polish stainless steel. See NRDC's This Green Life website, www.nrdc.org/thisgreenlife, for more information.
- Recycle and dispose of all trash properly. Never flush non-degradable products, such as disposable diapers or plastic tampon applicators, down the toilet. They can damage the sewage treatment process and end up littering beaches and waters.

- Conserve water. More than half of the water you use in your home is either flushed down the toilet or washed down the shower drain. Low-flow toilets and showerheads yield major water savings. Repair drips promptly; a dripping faucet can waste twenty gallons a day, a leaking toilet two hundred gallons.

IN YOUR YARD

- Apply natural fertilizer, such as compost, manure, bone meal, or peat, whenever possible. Composting decreases the need for fertilizer and helps soil retain moisture.
- Use slow-watering techniques on lawns and gardens. Over-watering lawns can increase the leaching of fertilizers into groundwater and runoff pollution into local waterways.
- Decrease impervious surfaces around your home. Landscape with vegetation, gravel, or other porous materials instead of cement. Redirect rain gutters and downspouts to soil, grass, or gravel areas. These techniques, called "green infrastructure," allow rainwater to replenish groundwater basins and keep runoff out of local waters.

MAINTAINING YOUR CAR

- Recycle used motor oil, and keep up on vehicle maintenance. Avoid pouring waste oil into gutters or down storm drains. A single quart of motor oil that seeps into groundwater can pollute 250,000 gallons of drinking water.
- Be "green" when washing your car. Hand wash your car with a bucket of soapy water, rags, and a hose. Just turning off the hose between rinsing can save up to 150 gallons.

IN YOUR COMMUNITY

- Be an activist! Contact your public officials and attend hearings to encourage them to support laws and programs to protect our water. For starters: every community in America should commit to using green infrastructure for new and redevelopment projects, and support water efficiency through utility incentive and credit programs. Join NRDC and visit our website for more information on what you can do to be part of the solution to our water challenges (www.nrdc.org/water). And follow us on Twitter for news and tips on everything water (@nrdcwater).

12

NINE ECOFABULOUS WAYS TO SAVE WATER AT HOME— AND DO IT WITH STYLE

Zem Joaquin

Zem Joaquin, founder of the ecofabulous website (www.ecofabulous.com), has been a contributing eco-editor at *House & Garden, Domino, Architectural Digest,* and *7×7* magazines. She received the 2009 Global Green Millennium Founder's Award for her contributions as a Global Green board member, cochair of Global Green's San Francisco committee, and founder of Global Green's successful annual fund-raiser and eco-fashion event. Mentored by architect and designer William McDonough, Joaquin is a certified BuildItGreen design and strategy consultant who helps companies and individuals create beautiful, smart, sustainable spaces and practices. Though she wears many hats, one of her favorites is the one she wears as eBay's eco expert.

Much of Joaquin's penchant for superior design came from her years at Splendora.com and living in Milan, Paris, and London. Her love for the earth, however, can be traced back to her early upbringing on a Palo Alto commune. As a mother of two, Joaquin is committed to improving all families' health, education, and access to well-vetted information. To that end Joaquin is an active board member of Global Green USA, Teens Turning Green, and the Cradle to Cradle Product Innovation Institute.

I created the website ecofabulous after realizing that many of the items I was using in my home were toxic and directly contributing to my children's asthma. To transform my own home into a healthy environment, I set out to educate myself about the products and materials I was using. The more I learned, the more passionate I became about sharing the healthier alternatives I was discovering. Inspired by my mentor William McDonough, whose Cradle to Cradle design philosophy has galvanized many leaders in business, science, and public policy, I created ecofabulous and the Zem's List newsletter to provide credible guidance for readers eager to find products and services that support a sustainable, abundant lifestyle.

Based in San Francisco, the site is devoted to inspiring and educating readers who don't want to compromise style or quality but seek the recommendations of expert editors and designers. We offer carefully vetted suggestions, guides, and newsletters featuring environmentally conscious beauty, fashion, home, kids, tech, and lifestyle products, along with conversational online and offline integrations, including interior design projects, brand programs with the likes of eBay, Levi's, and Intel, and curating of experiences such as the Modern Living Showhouse at Dwell on Design.

The unique perspective of ecofabulous is best captured in our manifesto:

Being *ecofabulous* means celebrating high style with low impact.

It's about beautiful items and experiences that don't compromise health but do inspire stares (the good, *where'd you get that from?* kind). We're obsessed with well-designed products. Yet our definition of beauty doesn't leave room for things that make you— or the planet—sick.

Being *ecofabulous* means being savvy and open for a bit of discovery.

It means being an expert on your options. It means understanding where your products are from, what they're made of, and what they will become in their next life—whether that be jeans, lipstick, or baby bottles.

Being *ecofabulous* doesn't mean sacrificing or smelling of patchouli oil, but it does mean inspiring change.

We search from Portugal to Palo Alto to bring you the best beauty, fashion, and home finds for a considered life. Though sustainability is at the top of our criteria, it's sitting right next to aesthetics, efficacy, and performance.

We take our product criteria seriously (but ourselves less so). We run on copious amounts of organic green tea and fair trade coffee, but only take it to go when we've remembered our own mugs. We've learned that well-made items are the healthiest and most desirable, and we're here to share them with you.

We're strong supporters of the message of the film *Last Call at the Oasis,* so when the editor of this companion book called to invite us to prepare a contribution, we were excited to participate. In the pages that follow, we'll offer nine of our favorite tips for people who want to improve the way they use water at home to conserve, protect, and defend this most precious of resources—and to do it without sacrificing comfort, pleasure, or style.

I. SWITCH TO GREEN CLEANING PRODUCTS THAT WON'T POLLUTE GROUNDWATER AND OTHER ECOSYSTEMS

A great first step to "greening" your life is to change your cleaning products—the chemicals we use every day on counters, cabinets, floors, tubs, toilets, windows, and elsewhere around the house and the office. Conventional cleaning products contain carcinogens and skin irritants, and their runoff contaminates soil, waterways, and other ecosystems. But switching to the traditional do-it-yourself vinegar and water solution is not always realistic (nor does it always smell that great).

Fortunately, complete lines of eco-friendly cleaning products are available nearly everywhere that work as well as their toxic counterparts, or even better. Some of my favorite lines are readily available in big-box chains as well as online: Method, Seventh Generation, and Bright Green are among the best. These products are made from biodegradable, plant-based ingredients derived from coconuts, essential oils, lemon, and corn, and come in recyclable (and often recycled) bottles.

2. USE A WATER FILTERING SYSTEM INSTEAD OF BOTTLED WATER FOR DRINKING

Health and beauty experts often recommend drinking eight glasses of water per day. But that can be hard to do, especially when the stuff that flows from your tap tastes like tires or old pipes. And nowadays, in too many locations, residues like heavy metals and pharmaceuticals are being found in the tap water. It's a real concern—not just a matter of taste, but potentially a risk to your health and that of your family.

Many people have turned to bottled water as a solution. But bottled water is costly, carries its own environmental costs (especially in the millions of tons of non-biodegradable plastic that is dumped into the ecosystem every year), and often is no safer than what flows from your kitchen sink. So, where to turn?

At ecofabulous, we suggest going back to tap water, which eliminates the need to manufacture and dispose of plastic bottles. The downside of tap water can be minimized by choosing an efficient filtering system, which will ensure that the water you drink is as tasty as can be, as well as free of bacteria and chemical residues. Here are some of the high-quality filtration systems we've recommended to our readers in recent months:

- We used Everpure's ViruPure filtration system in the 2010 Modern Living Showhouse at Dwell on Design and were really pleased with the results. Its thorough water purification and reduction of filter replacements impressed a steady stream of attendees; the patented technology is "like packing nearly six filters into one canister." We used the filtered water in the Sodastream system for a carbonated treat. The ViruPure system filters more than 99 percent of even the smallest possible viruses, bacteria, and microscopic giardia cysts from drinking water, and just one filter will last a family of four more than a year, replacing approximately 3,786 plastic water bottles, for a savings of about $3,270.

- The Ovopur is a filtration system of superior aesthetics, having received the "Best Product of the Year" award in the kitchen appliance category at the Guggenheim Museum's Interior Design Best of Year Awards in 2009. But what's beauty without the scientific backing? With such first-class filtering materials as KDF 55 (a highly regarded filtration medium made from an alloy of copper and zinc), activated carbon, microporous bioceramics, and quartz crystal, the multilayer Aquacristal filter cartridge is proven to remove chemicals and organic pollutants from your drinking water. What's more, the wireless system uses gravity instead of electricity to filter water and boasts the only glass filter we know of— so it's reusable, recyclable, and entirely free of plastic. The ceramic egg shape allows water to circulate inside to prevent stagnation and reduces bacteria buildup, plus the natural thermal properties of the ceramic keep the water surprisingly cool. And because it requires no electricity, you can move the stand around and place it wherever you'd like (great for outdoor parties in the summer and for renters— take it with you when you move). At $699, it's definitely an initial investment, but think of it like a great piece of furniture: you'll have that beauty for life. Additional filters run $59 and last for four months.

- The Zuvo Water Purator uses a patented five-step purification process with ultraviolet light to provide clean, delicious water straight from the tap. Though the upfront cost of $299 is significant, it will save you money in the long run, since each filter lasts for five hundred gallons and you receive an additional filter free with your Purator.

- Another elegant solution is the TriFlow integrated water filtration system from Rohl Home. Produced in the UK to the highest quality standards, it provides hot and cold filtered water from one faucet—plus an optional side spray. Each filter produces 1,000 gallons of water (that's the equivalent of 7,576 plastic water bottles). The system is also available for bathrooms as a Triflow Lavatory Faucet, so you can brush those pearly whites, gargle, and swallow with sparkling-fresh H_2O.

- We would be remiss if we did not mention the option of a whole-house filter. It involves a much larger investment but it is very rewarding if you can afford it. With a whole-house filter like the Wellness system, every tap in your house becomes a delightful drinking fountain—and the multi-thousand-dollar investment means that you won't have to change filters for seven years.

Whichever filter you opt for, remember to keep a stock of reusable containers to keep hydrated throughout the day. Three options to consider:

- Life Factory and BKR make bright, silicone-protected glass bottles.

- The shatterproof options we prefer are Earthlust (scintillating personal designs) and Kleen Kanteen for stainless steel sipping.
- Sippy cups have finally grown up—check out Innobaby's stainless toteable. Life Factory also makes colorful and safe baby bottles and sippy cup attachments.

3. INSTALL A FOOT PEDAL
TO CONTROL YOUR SINK FAUCET

When I'm asked about inexpensive but high-impact upgrades for the home, my go-to recommendation is a foot pedal for your sink. The valves are the same as those installed in hospitals and doctors' offices, designed to reduce the risk of exposure to *E. coli,* salmonella, and other nasty contaminants. And by using toe control, you run the water only when you really need it, not continuously, as so many of us do because of (bad) habits or because we don't want to dirty the handle.

Pedal valves cost under $200 and are very easy to install (though if you aren't handy, I recommend you call a plumber). And just think of the money you will save in water and the health benefits of not getting sick. The brand I have used is from www.PedalValve.com.

4. INSTALL A SMARTTOUCH FAUCET
FOR EASY-ON, EASY-OFF WATER FLOW

Another way to reduce water wastage at the tap is to use one of the new SmartTouch faucets by Brizo. No need to use a handle—simply touch anywhere on the faucet body to turn the water on or off. It's as simple as that. You don't have to contaminate the fixture with dirty hands, and you're much more likely to turn the water off and conserve than if you have to fiddle with the controls each time.

5. CUT DOWN ON UNCONSCIOUS WATER WASTE IN THE BATHROOM

Did you know that 75 percent of the water we use at home is used in the bathroom? It's a startling statistic, but that means it can be easy to enjoy big savings, just by being aware of your behavior every time you step into your tiled sanctuary. Here are some specific tips that can cut down water waste without sacrificing ease or comfort:

- Don't leave the water running while you brush your teeth or wash your face and hands—it wastes one gallon per minute.
- Don't use the toilet as a trash receptacle—toss tissues or other small items in the wastepaper basket rather than flushing them down the drain. A toilet can use up to seven gallons of water per flush.
- Shorten your showers. Use an egg timer to remind yourself to wash quickly and efficiently—or if you like to shower to your favorite music, try to limit yourself to the length of just one song. Cutting down your average shower time by just one minute can save around a thousand gallons of water per year.

6. SWITCH TO A WATER-SAVING TOILET MODEL

Next time you need to replace a toilet, put water conservation at the top of your priority list. A dual-flush system, which uses less water for liquid waste and more for the solid stuff (but still less than typical new commodes), provides greater efficiency with no aesthetic sacrifice. And you may get a rebate that will offset any additional up-front costs.

Some manufacturers are creating even more ingenious water-saving innovations. One of the leaders in the field, the Australian-based Caroma, offers the Profile toilet, which boasts an integrated hand basin where freshwater is first used to wash hands before flowing into the cistern to be used to flush the toilet. The streamlined design saves space (it's perfect for a compact powder room) and still includes a dual-flush button for additional water savings.

7. OR CONSIDER A SELF-COMPOSTING TOILET FOR EVEN GREATER SAVINGS

With over 90 percent of all toilet waste being water, you can save up to 75,000 gallons of water each year by using a self-composting toilet—leading to big savings on your water bill. The remaining 10 percent of toilet waste is organic material that can be recycled into natural compost with very little effort. Though a self-composting toilet does run more than a traditional toilet (ranging in price from $1,700 to $6,000), your reduced water bill will offset the cost dramatically when amortized over time. And some of the latest models combine high style with eco efficiency. We recently recommended a self-composting toilet in hot pink from Envirolet that is sure to provoke the right kind of potty talk in any home.

8. MAKE YOUR NEXT WASHING MACHINE A WATER-SAVING, ECO-FRIENDLY MODEL

The newest washing machines offer an astounding array of features that combine technology, high style, and efficiency—including impressive water savings—without any loss of cleaning effectiveness. The 2011 Electrolux washer and dryer are incredibly efficient across the board. The enormous capacity allows for massively condensed loads: you can fit comforters, multiple sheet sets, and bulky towels all in the same load, and fewer loads mean less water. But if you have less to wash, it will adjust for that, too. An entire wash and dry cycle can be completed in just about thirty minutes. Available in an array of gleaming hues, it is my favorite appliance in the house. Another good option is the Vantage washer from Whirlpool, which features sleek curved styling (reminiscent of a high-performance car), an LCD touch screen with vibrant color images, the industry's first USB ports as well as customizable laundry cycles, and a Stain Assist option designed to help you get out tough stains.

Even if you can't afford to change out your washing machine, you can save a ton of water in the laundry room by switching to highly concentrated detergent. Size does matter! Method recently released its liquid that is eight times more concentrated than conventional detergent, which dramatically cuts down on packaging, water waste, and transportation. It also means you won't injure yourself lugging around oversized containers. Alternatively, Seventh Generation has introduced a four-times concentrate packaged in Ecologic's smart biodegradable fiber. And remember, line-drying your wash is one of the easiest, most impactful ways to reduce your home's carbon footprint.

9. INSTALL A RAINWATER CAPTURE AND STORAGE SYSTEM

The idea of harvesting rainwater for use in the home is tremendously appealing, but for most urban dwellers it has long seemed impractical. Now, however, Sydney-based architect Sally Dominguez has designed the Rainwater HOG, a modular water storage unit small enough for urbanites. You can also install a larger array in a suburban or rural setting.

The Rainwater HOG can be installed vertically or horizontally (it's great under decks and in narrow passages). It holds up to fifty-one gallons of rainwater, collected via a downspout attached to the roof. Should you need more storage, simply add another HOG. Made of food-grade plastic, the modular structure is entirely recyclable. At $350 to $465 per unit (depending on your choice of accessories), the initial cost is easily recouped over time as you wash your car and water your plants without adding to your utility bill—not to mention the added savings for the planet.

The Rainwater HOG gives a whole new meaning to the expression "rainy day fund"!

––––––

The best news is that these nine ideas are just the tip of the iceberg. Creative entrepreneurs and increasingly savvy major corporations are continually coming up with new products designed to help save the planet while enhancing our daily lives. So please visit ecofabulous and sign up for Zem's List to stay current on the latest great ideas—and let us know how you're transforming your life through smarter, stylish, sustainable design solutions.

13

"ENDLESS RESOURCEFULNESS"

A Conversation About Water
with William McDonough

William McDonough is a globally recognized leader in sustainable development. Trained as an architect, McDonough has a wide range of interests and influence, and he works at scales from the global to the molecular. *Time* magazine recognized him in 1999 as a "Hero for the Planet," stating that "his utopianism is grounded in a unified philosophy that—in demonstrable and practical ways—is changing the design of the world." In 1996 McDonough received the Presidential Award for Sustainable Development, the nation's highest environmental honor, and in 2003 he earned the first US EPA Presidential Green Chemistry Challenge Award for his work with Shaw Industries, the carpet division of Berkshire Hathaway. In 2004 he received the National Design Award for exemplary achievement in environmental design. McDonough is the architect of many of the recognized flagships of sustainable design, including Ford's River Rouge Plant in Dearborn, Michigan; the Adam Joseph Lewis Center for Environmental Studies at Oberlin College; and NASA's new space station on Earth, Sustainability Base, completed in 2011.

He has written and lectured extensively on design as the first signal of human intention, everywhere and at all scales. His firm was commissioned in 1991 to create the Hannover Principles: Design for Sustainability as guidelines for the City of Hannover's EXPO 2000 (in Germany), still recognized as the touchstone of sustainable design. McDonough and Michael Braungart cowrote *Cradle to Cradle: Remaking the Way We Make Things* (2002), which is widely acknowledged as one of the seminal texts of the sustainability movement.

McDonough advises major enterprises including commercial and governmental leaders worldwide through McDonough Advisors. He also is active with William McDonough + Partners, his architecture practice, with offices in Charlottesville, Virginia, and San Francisco, as well as McDonough Braungart Design Chemistry, the Cradle to Cradle assessment and consulting firm cofounded with Braungart. With Braungart, he has cofounded not-for-profit organizations to allow public accessibility of Cradle to Cradle thinking; these include GreenBlue (2000), to convene industry groups around Cradle to Cradle issues, and the Cradle to Cradle Products Innovation Institute, founded at the invitation of California Governor Arnold Schwarzenegger to create a global standard for the development of safe and healthy products. McDonough and Braungart contributed the Cradle to Cradle certification program to the institute. McDonough also cofounded Make It Right (2006) with Brad Pitt to bring affordable Cradle to Cradle–inspired homes to the Lower 9th Ward Institute of New Orleans after Hurricane Katrina.

In December 2011, editor Karl Weber and McDonough spoke about his work in relation to water. "Endless Resourcefulness"—a term McDonough celebrates and applies to resources and people's creativity—is a selection of McDonough's remarks from that conversation.

I turned sixty in 2011. I'm from the Far East originally—born in Tokyo in 1951, and then I lived in Hong Kong until I was a teen. In Hong Kong in the late '50s and early '60s, we had numerous water crises during the dry seasons (it was before the building of a pipeline from China). I learned part of what it means to be without water—often. Sometimes our part of the island was supplied with water for just four hours every fourth day. That was it—no such thing as turning a tap and getting a seemingly endless stream of safe water from a municipal supply. And so we collected rainwater in cisterns and had to boil it to drink. We filled every kind of container we could find. We filled glasses and pots and bowls and especially KLIM cans, the old powdered-milk cans that the British had sent to their citizens overseas during the Second World War. Those KLIM cans—"klim" is "milk," spelled backward—became the ubiquitous bucket in the

Far East and a source of sheet metal for making thousands of objects. And when the city pipes were turned on, all of us in our household would volunteer to line up for water at the public taps. It's amazing to think back to those times.

So, yes, I see water as precious. But limited? No, that might not be the only way to think about it. I don't just see water as limited. I see water as being of endless resourcefulness, but it needs our care, and it needs us to celebrate its resourcefulness as a material and our creative use of it—not simply to bemoan it as a limited thing that is being destroyed by human abuse or human-induced climate change.

When you simply think of water as limited, then instead of tapping its endless potential for sharing and recirculation in hydrologic cycles, your mind gets channeled into thoughts about simply being "less bad" in our treatment of this essential life-giving, even life-defining resource. We start thinking: be more efficient, dump fewer toxics in water, and so on—and while these are obviously well-meaning and certainly worthwhile actions, they are not necessarily the most beneficial path to life and health. Thinking this way may just be embarking on the path to slower death.

And so my work as a change agent begins with challenging people's perceptions. It begins with realigning a few brain cells and getting people to think about things they may not have thought about. Things like drinking their urine.

I can hear you saying "Yuck!" and I understand that reaction. But at the NASA Sustainability Base in California, which we designed with the space agency, they have a system like those on the space stations that can allow the "terranauts" (in this instance) to recycle water—all of it, including urine if they wish. The building's systems use filtering membranes similar to the ones that are used in space stations in geosynchronous orbit 22,000 miles above the surface of the earth to purify what people tend to call "waste products" and turn them into potable water. We have similar systems for energy, air supply, heat, and cooling, designing what I call this earth-bound "space station" in geosynchronous orbit on terra firma as if it were a self-sufficient space station.

But perhaps a better comparison is to a tree. It's a building that is alive and that participates in the natural flow of resources just like any natural, living thing. If your reaction is still "Yuck!" then I'd suggest you get over it. Because this is the way we need to think and design our environment for a planet of 10 billion people (which the UN expects us to be inhabiting by midcentury).

Singapore has already gotten over the yuck factor. They take all their sewer water, convert it back into H_2O, suck out the phosphates and nitrates and scum, and return it to potable quality. They call it "new water." How wonderful a way to use the language to overcome perceived aversions—who wants old water anyway?—and everybody's happy. Isn't it fascinating what changing the *name* can do? That's the power of realigning those brain cells.

Meanwhile, cities like San Diego and Sydney have gone through intense debates about their water protocols. In San Diego, those who advocated a system like the one in Singapore were calling it "indirect potable reuse," while those who hated the concept used the phrase "toilet-to-tap," which activated everybody's "Yuck" synapses. So what did they end up doing instead? They pump the sewage down into the ground and then suck it out months later. They call it "ground water." Do you see what they're doing? It's the same water, just filtered a little bit by *terra firma,* and that makes people feel better. It's just good old H_2O.

Perceptions are important. I think we should do whatever it takes within our wonderfully diverse cultures. We have to manage technology, we have to manage perceptions, and we have to choose the words we use with care. But personally I like talking about drinking our urine, because it makes the design challenge very vivid and unmistakable. I like to think we're grown up enough to face it, get over the "Yuck" factor, and move on to better things.

The larger point is that water is not just a content—it's also a currency, it's flow. It's flow of money, flow of people, flow of health, flow of fecundity. Water is a medium that makes all life possible—the magical vehicle that catalyzes the energy of the sun with the materials of the earth and helps it all become biology. That's what water is for us. The flow of water means that we can exist. It has to do with almost everything living, it touches everything—it's so beautiful. So when you mess with water, you're messing with everything.

And why have we been messing with this precious living medium of water? Bad design. We poop, we pollute. We mine, we pollute. We farm, we pollute. We make things, we pollute. We create so many materials that we insist on thinking of as "waste" products and then we dump them into our rivers, streams, lakes, and oceans. It's awfully stupid, really.

But to change the system, you need to start by changing the way you think. We've found ways to convert what people normally call "sewage plants" into "nutrient management systems." We can suck out the phosphates and the nitrates and the other dissolved minerals that are essential for life, and now we have a fertilizer product that can be sold to farmers and earn a 12 percent rate of return. It makes so much sense as a business proposition. Instead of building a waste disposal plant that people think of as a liability for the community— a costly, ugly, smelly thing nobody wants in their backyard and an expensive drain on local resources—we eliminate the *concept* of waste. Everything we conventionally think of as waste is really a nutrient, an asset. So we shift the traditional thinking about design from asset-to-liability to asset-to-asset. This is the Cradle to Cradle thinking that I have developed with Dr. Michael Braungart, instead of the traditional cradle-to-grave thinking.

It's the same principle a tree works on. And then if we want to release the purified water from our nutrient management plant into the nearby bay or estuary, there's no problem; it's clean and refreshing to the ecosystem instead of degrading and damaging.

Of course, it's not *just* a matter of perceptions. It's a matter of technology and design as well. We've lately been working with the Dutch on many fronts and are enjoying watching them develop new systems for phosphorous recovery from sewage plants. One of my favorite examples of this idea originated in a waste treatment plant in Vancouver. A mechanic was trying to make sure the pipes didn't clog up from the gradual mineralization of the solids flowing through the pipes—a little like the way your tea kettle at home gets crusty over time. It is my understanding that a scientist named Donald S. Mavinic tried putting these materials in a vortex to separate out the minerals. He found that they came out in little round mineral spheres—beautiful things, actually. The resulting product is called struvite, and it's mostly phosphate, a tiny bit of magnesium, and some nitrogen, and it's a profitable, valuable fertilizer.

And a lot of the solutions we should be looking at focus simply on *where* we do things. Maybe we ought to start building vertical farming and greenhouses right on the back of our nutrient management systems (former sewage treatment sites), so that the dissolved minerals necessary to plant growth are already in the water that's delivered to them for super-productive hydroponic agriculture. Our reliance on imported essential minerals would go way down as a result—and hydroponic agriculture can raise the same volume of produce as traditional farming while using just 8 percent of the water. Cities could deliver food and fertilizer, clean water, economic benefits, and jobs while eliminating point-source pollutions, all the while benefiting farmers by providing valuable slow-release fertilizers that eliminate non-point-source pollution in the countryside.

But in the meantime we're still stuck between old and new ways of thinking. One of the basic protocols of the Industrial Revolution started in the eighteenth and nineteenth centuries, it appears to me, is the idea that if brute force isn't working, you're not using enough of it. So our solution to many problems has been to use more energy and water and to pour on more concrete. If we keep thinking that way, the results over the next few decades will be an extension of what we have been seeing more and more: tragic consequences.

Instead, why not design our cities as organisms? Why not design our cities to feed themselves and to cycle water continually? Why can't we run the gray water people have used for cleaning through simple sand filters and membranes and then use it, building by building, for irrigation and vertical agriculture? Why can't we use the new LED lighting to grow fruits and vegetables using only the essential parts of the visible spectrum, which require a fraction of the energy needed for white light? Yes, these technologies are available today, and they work. We can grow sweet strawberries as big as your fist if we want to—and without even thinking about transgenic genetically modified organisms.

But shifting our thinking is hard. Look at what China—a highly populated country with a hyperactive economy—is doing. According to some, only 10 percent of China's vast land mass is desirable, and its government is most concerned about how they're going to feed the hundreds of millions of new people that are arriving in the next few decades. As has been typical in western farming, the first reaction is to apply brute force: Let's develop genetically modified seeds to force increased crop yields; let's amp up our systems of conventional agriculture, even though we find ourselves watching the plowed-up soil blow away or no-till farming aggregating herbicides in the soil and binding minerals.

What agendas result from this mind-set? Shall we move a lot more water to dry places, even if that means diverting rivers and building gigantic dams that will make the Three Gorges project look like a Lego toy? And just in case all of this doesn't work, shall we consider buying farmland on other continents? What about buying land and mines in Africa and South America, figuring that is perhaps how we can hope to feed the next generation of children? It has often been said that insanity can be defined as doing the same thing over and over and expecting different results.

What if there were a change in thinking from the bottom up— a very different vision based on a new design model? What about increasing agricultural productivity at home by 20 percent—not just on farms, but in cities, which can go a long way toward feeding themselves, dramatically reducing the need for trucks and trains to transport produce over hundreds, even thousands of miles. We can extract the nutrients from used water that's already available in the cities and use them to grow food in magnificent vertical farms. We can drive it all using solar power and wind power, which are actually available in abundance. It's a matter of design, and of connecting dots we have not seen connected before. What if wind equaled food on the loess plains of Shanxi? All these innovations are already in the works.

It's time for a heavy dose of common sense combined with optimized economic, social, and ecological systems thinking. With this kind of thinking, goals become clear and powerful, centered on being "more good" instead of being "less bad." The re-envisioning of current practice is so clear and so powerful. But we need people to clear their minds to accept it.

There's an old joke about a third-grade teacher who tells her students, "Kids, let's all draw what we love today. Mary, what are you going to draw?"

Mary replies, "I'm going to draw a picture of God."

The teacher says, "You can't draw a picture of God. Nobody knows what God looks like."

And Mary answers, "I know. That's why I have to draw my picture."

So let's have the confidence to start drawing pictures. Let's try together to let people everywhere see how creative and generous we all are and that we can have regenerative systems instead of degenerative ones. Everything we need, including abundant water, is right here, available to us.

And the beauty really is that none of these ideas are alien to human tradition—or even specifically to China. They've been farming for forty centuries. How do you farm for 4,000 years without a chemical industry? You understand nutrient and water flow, that's how.

The reality is that we don't have a water problem, we don't have an energy problem. We have plenty of water and plenty of energy. We have a resources-in-the-wrong-place problem.

Take carbon, for example. Carbon emissions from the burning of fossil fuels are contributing massively to global climate change. And a lot of the carbon we're producing ends up in the oceans. Forty-three percent of anthropogenic carbon is now in the oceans, which means that the oceans are going acidic. We know that for ages the pH level of the oceans has ranged between 8.8 and 8.2. It's now on the way to 7.9. At 7.9, we're heading for carbonic acid, and mollusks can't form shells, which means by the end of the century we'll probably have destroyed the bottom of the food chain in the water. Really, really dumb.

But does this means we have a "carbon problem"? Of course not. There's nothing wrong with carbon. It makes me sad to hear carbon demonized. We are carbon. If you don't like carbon, then you don't like life. It's just that we have carbon in the wrong place. Nature wants to use solar energy to grow biota and sequester carbon in the soil.

So let's celebrate carbon. Let's just put it in the right place, in us and in soil. And in the same spirit, let's celebrate the abundance of water. Our job is not to bemoan the limits of water. Our job is to celebrate the infinite fecundity, richness, and resourcefulness of water, and to be smart about how we use it.

It's so simple. It's common sense. It's humbling. And so huge. The challenge is endless—but, then, that's the point.

Part III | GETTING INVOLVED

RESOURCES FOR LEARNING AND ACTIVISM

A. ORGANIZATIONS WORKING TO PROTECT AND IMPROVE OUR WATER SUPPLY

ALLIANCE FOR WATER EFFICIENCY

www.allianceforwaterefficiency.org
A nonprofit organization dedicated to the efficient and sustainable use of water in the United States and Canada. Its program activities include performing water-efficiency policy advocacy at the state and national levels, offering conservation program assistance at the community water-system level, providing support for water-efficient codes and standards, ensuring that water-efficient products are accessible, educating consumers, training water conservation professionals, and offering water-efficiency education at the individual consumer level. A separate website provides detailed information to the consumer on reducing wasteful water use in the home, including a calculator that measures the conserved water savings in terms of water and energy use as well as in dollars.

AMERICAN RIVERS

www.amrivers.org
American Rivers is a national group with local offices nationwide focused on conservation of rivers for environmental protection,

economic development, flood management, river restoration and protection, wetlands protection, clean municipal waste and storm water, water efficiency, and climate change adaptation.

ARCHITECTURE FOR HUMANITY

www.architectureforhumanity.org
Architecture for Humanity is a nonprofit design services firm founded in 1999. It is building a more sustainable future through the power of professional design.

By tapping a network of more than 50,000 professionals willing to lend time and expertise to help those who otherwise could not afford their services, the firm brings design, construction, and development services where they are most critically needed.

ARID LANDS INSTITUTE

http://aridlands.woodbury.edu
In a region pressed with water scarcity challenges, Arid Lands Institute offers a unique approach to addressing water conservation by working with designers, architects, and engineers to rethink and redesign the built environment in the western United States to better capture and conserve water resources. This macro approach is bringing new ideas and training to leaders, college and graduate students, and research fellows across disciplines, and has the potential to make the western United States a global leader, not a follower, in water conservation practices.

CALIFORNIA AGRICULTURAL WATER STEWARDSHIP INITIATIVE

http://agwaterstewards.org
The California Agricultural Water Stewardship Initiative aims to raise awareness about approaches to agricultural water management that support the viability of agriculture, conserve water, and protect ecological integrity in California. The organization works closely with farmers and irrigation districts to engage in water conservation practices.

CENTER FOR ENVIRONMENTAL HEALTH

www.ceh.org/about-us/mission
The Center for Environmental Health is working to eliminate the threat that synthetic chemicals pose to children, families, and communities.

CERES, AQUA GAUGE

www.ceres.org/issues/water/aqua-gauge
Ceres is a nonprofit organization that leads a national coalition of investors, environmental organizations, and other public interest groups working with companies to address sustainability challenges such as global climate change and water scarcity. *The Ceres Aqua Gauge: A Framework for 21st Century Water Risk Management* downloadable software application introduces a new framework and tool for assessing corporate water risk management. The Aqua Gauge focuses on governance and management, stakeholder engagement and disclosure.

CHARITY: WATER

www.charitywater.org
Charity: water is a nonprofit organization bringing clean and safe drinking water to people in developing nations. One hundred percent of public donations directly fund water projects.

CLEAN WATER AMERICA ALLIANCE

www.cleanwateramericaalliance.org
The 501(c)(3) nonprofit Clean Water America Alliance is exploring the complex issue of water sustainability and planning for the future by improving public awareness that advances holistic, watershed-based approaches to water quality and quantity challenges. A broad cross-section of interests have come together through the alliance to begin an important dialogue on the future, focusing on exploring and analyzing issues of critical importance to the nation's ability to provide clean and safe water to future generations, offering information and education to citizens and policy makers on key issues, and recognizing organizations and individuals for innovation and outstanding achievements in water quality and quantity.

CLEAN WATER NETWORK

www.cleanwaternetwork.org
The Clean Water Network is a national coalition of more than 1,200 local, state, and national nonprofit public interest organizations working to protect the health, safety, and quality of the nation's waters. It is the largest advocacy coalition in the country working to protect the nation's water resources. The mission of the Clean Water

Network is to work together to protect and restore clean water and wetlands throughout the nation. The Clean Water Network's goal is to safeguard water quality for future generations by working to defend, strengthen, and implement the Clean Water Act. The network is also very active on water quantity and supply issues, working to address the serious effects on our nation's water resources from global warming.

COMMUNITY ENVIRONMENTAL LEGAL DEFENSE FUND

www.celdf.org
The Community Environmental Legal Defense Fund is a nonprofit, public interest law firm providing free and affordable legal services to communities facing threats to their local environment, local agriculture, the local economy, and their quality of life. The fund's mission is to build sustainable communities by helping people assert their right to local self-government and the rights of nature.

CONSORTIUM OF UNIVERSITIES FOR THE ADVANCEMENT OF HYDROLOGIC SCIENCE INC.

www.cuahsi.org
The Consortium of Universities for the Advancement of Hydrologic Science (CUAHSI) enables the university water-science community to advance understanding of the central role of water to life, Earth, and society. CUAHSI focuses on water from bedrock to atmosphere, from summit to sea, and from the geologic past through the present and into the future.

CRADLE TO CRADLE

www.c2ccertified.org
The Cradle to Cradle Products Innovation Institute is a nonprofit organization whose mission is to bring about a large-scale transformation in the way manufacturers and designers make safe and healthy products for our world.

DEFENDERS OF WILDLIFE

www.defenders.org
Defenders of Wildlife is a national nonprofit membership organization dedicated to protecting all native animals and plants in their natural communities. It works to protect and restore America's native wildlife, safeguard habitat, resolve conflicts, work across international borders, and educate and mobilize the public.

DROP IN THE BUCKET

www.dropinthebucket.org
Drop in the Bucket (DITB) is a Los Angeles–based water charity that constructs wells and sanitation systems at large rural schools in sub-Saharan Africa. Since forming in 2006, the organization has completed over 150 projects in six countries there. DITB was formed by a group of entertainment industry professionals who decided to do something about the fact that every day, children in Africa are dying of preventable water-borne diseases. To that end, the staff has worked directly with individual communities to design and build cost-effective wells and innovative sanitation systems at local schools.

ENVIRONMENT AMERICA

www.environmentamerica.org
Environment America is a federation of state-based, citizen-funded environmental advocacy organizations. It's a national organization with state chapters across the country, working on water conservation and protection. It combines independent research, practical ideas, and tough-minded advocacy to overcome the opposition of powerful special interests. Environment America draws on thirty years of success in tackling environmental problems.

ENVIRONMENTAL DEFENSE FUND

www.edf.org
The Environmental Defense Fund's mission is to preserve the natural systems on which all life depends. Guided by science, the fund designs and transforms markets to bring lasting solutions to the most serious environmental problems.

ENVIRONMENTAL JUSTICE COALITION FOR WATER

www.ejcw.org
The Environmental Justice Coalition for Water, a coalition organization, works in the most underserved communities in California, most of which have highly contaminated water and/or no access to potable water. The group works to organize local residents to become advocates of better water policies.

ENVIRONMENTAL
MEDIA ASSOCIATION

www.ema-online.org
The Environmental Media Association (EMA) believes that through television, film, and music, the entertainment community has the power to influence the environmental awareness of millions of people. EMA mobilizes the entertainment industry in educating people about environmental issues, which in turn inspires them to take action.

ENVIRONMENTAL PROTECTION AGENCY
WATER SENSE LABEL PROGRAM

www.epa.gov/WaterSense
WaterSense, a partnership program by the US Environmental Protection Agency, seeks to protect the future of our nation's water supply by offering people a simple way to use less water with water-efficient products, new homes, and services. The program helps consumers make smart water choices that save money and maintain high environmental standards without compromising performance.

ENVIRONMENTAL WORKING GROUP

http://ewg.org
EWG is a leader in disseminating scientific research as digestible, actionable tools for consumers. The group works on privatization of bottled water, water pollutants, water subsidies, and the agriculture-water nexus. The group is also a key player in legislative advocacy in California and Washington, D.C., on water and related policies.

FOOD & WATER WATCH

www.foodandwaterwatch.org
Food & Water Watch is a nonprofit organization that advocates for commonsense policies that will result in healthy, safe food and access to safe and affordable drinking water. Its international staff in Latin America and the European Union (where the group is known as Food & Water Europe) works with coalition partners to track the global impact of US corporations on public policy. The organization works on a range of water issues, including bottled water, privatization, infrastructure, fracking, water pricing, national regulations, and legislation.

FRIENDS OF THE EARTH MIDDLE EAST

http://foeme.org
Friends of the Earth Middle East (FoEME) is a unique organization that brings together Jordanian, Palestinian, and Israeli environmentalists. Its primary objective is to promote cooperative efforts to protect our shared environmental heritage. In so doing, it seeks to advance both sustainable regional development and the creation of necessary conditions for lasting peace in the Middle East. FoEME has offices in Amman, Bethlehem, and Tel Aviv. FoEME is a member of Friends of the Earth International, the largest grassroots environmental organization in the world.

GLOBAL GREEN

www.globalgreen.org
Founded in 1993 by activist and philanthropist Diane Meyer Simon, Global Green USA is the American arm of Green Cross International, which was created by Mikhail Gorbachev to foster a

global value shift toward a sustainable and secure future by reconnecting humanity with the environment. Global Green is working to address some of the greatest challenges facing humanity. In the United States, the group primarily focuses on fighting global climate change through its green affordable-housing initiatives, National Green Schools Initiative, national and regional green building policies, advocacy, and education.

HEADSUP!

www.visualizing.org/partners/headsup
HeadsUp! is an international competition challenging designers to visualize critical global issues and create a shared sign for the public square. Working with global data on issues such as global groundwater levels, climate change, and ocean acidification, designers create a series of visual displays to translate abstract metrics into recognizable and actionable news. It is an opportunity to transform planetary data into a common sign combining the metaphorical power of the Doomsday Clock with the authority of data visualization and the immediacy of activist electronic billboards: a HeadsUp!

H_2O CONSERVE

www.h2oconserve.org
H_2O Conserve is an online source of tools and information that enable individuals to make water conservation part of their everyday lives, using this platform as an engaging, interactive consumer education tool about water conservation issues. It is a project of

GRACE, a nonprofit organization working on the connection between food, water, and energy.

THE HYDROLOGY
& CLIMATE RESEARCH GROUP

www.ess.uci.edu/~hydrogroup/index.html
The Hydrology & Climate Research Group in the Department of Earth System Science at the University of California at Irvine is the research group of Professor Jay Famiglietti. It focuses on modeling and remote sensing of the terrestrial and global water cycles. The group's work has implications for hydrologic- and earth-system modeling, for characterizing water cycle variability across multiple scales, for understanding its interactions in the land-ocean-atmosphere-ice system, and for monitoring changes in freshwater availability in the context of global environmental change. The group is composed of PhD students, postdoctoral researchers, and occasionally, highly motivated undergraduates. The projects range in scale and complexity from basin-scale field studies to integrated modeling and satellite studies of global hydrology.

IZAAK WALTON LEAGUE

www.iwla.org
Founded in 1922, the Izaak Walton League is one of the nation's oldest and most respected conservation organizations. With a powerful grassroots network of more than 250 local chapters nationwide, the league takes a commonsense approach to protecting our country's natural heritage and improving outdoor recreation opportunities for all Americans.

JANE GOODALL INSTITUTE

www.janegoodall.org
Founded by renowned primatologist Jane Goodall, the Jane Goodall Institute is a global nonprofit that empowers people to make a difference for all living things. The organization builds on Goodall's scientific work and her humanitarian vision. Specifically, it seeks to improve global understanding and treatment of great apes through research, public education, and advocacy.

NATIONAL GEOGRAPHIC

http://environment.nationalgeographic.com/environment/freshwater
The National Geographic Society's freshwater initiative is a multiyear global effort to inspire and empower individuals and communities to conserve freshwater and preserve the extraordinary diversity of life that rivers, lakes, and wetlands sustain.

NATIONAL SUSTAINABLE AGRICULTURE COALITION

http://sustainableagriculture.net
This coalition is working through the federal Farm Bill on conservation programs that affect water sources, including the Conservation Stewardship program, Environmental Quality Incentives program, Wetlands Reserve program, and Conservation Reserve program. This alliance of organizations representing small and medium-size farms across the United States promotes legislation for the sustainability of agriculture, rural communities, and food systems.

NATURAL RESOURCES DEFENSE COUNCIL

www.nrdc.org
The Natural Resources Defense Council is the nation's most effective environmental action group, combining the grassroots power of 1.3 million members and online activists with the courtroom clout and expertise of more than 350 lawyers, scientists, and other professionals. The organization is a leader in regional and national legislation and regulation advocacy and focuses on green infrastructure, water efficiency, and climate change modeling.

THE NATURE CONSERVANCY

http://prod.nature.org
The Nature Conservancy is the leading conservation organization working around the world to protect ecologically important lands and waters for nature and people. The organization is working on six hundred watershed projects nationally and internationally, especially focused on climate change, freshwater, oceans, infrastructure, impacts, and pollution.

ONE DROP

www.onedrop.org
One Drop is an initiative of Guy Laliberté, founder of Cirque du Soleil in Montreal, Canada. One Drop is a charitable organization that develops integrated, innovative projects with an international scope, in which water plays a central role as a creative force in generating positive, sustainable effects for local and foreign populations and in the fight against poverty.

PACIFIC INSTITUTE

www.pacinst.org
Perhaps the world's leading independent research and policy think tank addressing global freshwater challenges, strategy, and policy. Founder and president Peter Gleick is a MacArthur "Genius" Fellowship winner and a member of the US Academy of Sciences. The organization offers a plethora of resources and research on a host of water issues to inform decision makers, advocates, and the general public. It also produces the biennial water report *The World's Water*, published by Island Press.

PESTICIDE ACTION NETWORK

http://panna.org
Pesticide Action Network (PAN) North America works to replace the use of hazardous pesticides with ecologically sound and socially just alternatives. As one of five PAN regional centers worldwide, the North America branch links local and international consumer, labor, health, environmental, and agricultural groups into an international citizens' action network.

RIVERKEEPER

www.riverkeeper.org
Riverkeeper works to protect the environmental, recreational, and commercial integrity of the Hudson River and its tributaries, and to safeguard the drinking water of 9 million New York City and Hudson River Valley residents.

SALMON-SAFE

www.salmonsafe.org
Started by an environmental group, this Pacific Northwest organization offers Salmon-Safe certification to consumer products that protect wild salmon by preserving habitats, conserving water, phasing out pesticides, replacing urban areas with native plants, and planting climate-appropriate crops.

THE SAMBURU PROJECT

www.thesamburuproject.org
Founded in 2005 by Kristen Kosinski, the nonprofit Samburu Project collaborates with communities in developing countries to enhance the daily lives of men, women, and children by providing resources that address immediate needs while promoting long-term sustainability and self-sufficiency along with cultural integrity. The Samburu Project's primary goal is to provide easy access to clean, safe drinking water in communities throughout the Samburu district of Kenya.

SIERRA CLUB

http://sierraclub.org
Sierra Club water sentinels work to protect, improve, and restore our waters by fostering alliances to promote water quality monitoring, public education, and citizen action. Lynn Henning of the Michigan Sierra Club is heavily featured in the film *Last Call at the Oasis* for her CAFO work.

SKOLL FOUNDATION

www.skollfoundation.org
The Skoll Foundation drives large-scale change by investing in, connecting, and celebrating social entrepreneurs and the innovators who help them solve the world's most pressing problems. By identifying the people and programs already bringing positive change around the world, the foundation empowers them to extend their reach, deepen their impact, and fundamentally improve society.

THE SKOLL GLOBAL THREATS FUND

www.skollglobalthreats.org
The Skoll Global Threats Fund's mission is to confront global threats imperiling humanity by seeking solutions, strengthening alliances, and spurring actions needed to safeguard the future. It works to find, initiate, or cocreate breakthrough ideas and/or activities that it believes will have large-scale impact, either directly or indirectly, and whether on cross-cutting issues or individual threats.

UNIVERSITY OF CALIFORNIA CENTER FOR HYDROLOGIC MODELING

www.ucchm.org/Site/Welcome.html
The University of California Center for Hydrologic Modeling is an initiative across nearly all the UC campuses and affiliated laboratories to create a state-of-the-art, integrated model of California water resources. The founding director since fall 2009, Professor Jay Famiglietti, additionally holds appointments in the Departments of Earth System Science, and Civil and Environmental Engineering at the University of California at Irvine.

US GEOLOGICAL SURVEY

www.usgs.gov
The mission of the Geomagnetism Program is to monitor the earth's magnetic field. Using ground-based observatories, the program provides continuous records of magnetic-field variations covering long time scales; disseminates magnetic data to various governmental, academic, and private institutions; and conducts research into the nature of geomagnetic variations for purposes of scientific understanding and hazard mitigation.

VIRTUAL WATER

www.virtual-water.org
The Virtual Water project shows the world how much freshwater is used to produce selected products—and help people rethink their consumption patterns. Designer Timm Kekeritz created a set of info graphics, visualizing parts of their research data, to make the issue of virtual water and the water footprint perceptible.

WATER DEFENSE

www.waterdefense.org
Water Defense works to protect our water from the destruction of dirty fossil fuel industries by promoting clean energy policies and empowering people to protect their watersheds. Founded by actor Mark Ruffalo, Water Defense engages renowned cultural figures, produces educational events, and informs the public through traditional and social media to raise awareness, drive policy change, and end America's fossil fuel addiction by demanding sustainable solutions.

WATER FOR PEOPLE

www.waterforpeople.org
Water for People helps people in developing countries improve quality of life by supporting the development of locally sustainable drinking water resources, sanitation facilities, and hygiene education programs.

WATER IN THE WEST

http://waterinthewest.stanford.edu
Water in the West is a joint program of the Woods Institute for the Environment and the Bill Lane Center for the American West at Stanford University. Water in the West is engaging in a strategically designed set of research and policy initiatives to develop and demonstrate solutions to the major water challenges facing the western United States. The challenges are formidable. The problems and their solutions have complicated technical and institutional dimensions. That is why the program has assembled a strong interdisciplinary team of researchers at Stanford University, along with partners from other universities and the public and private sectors. This team will address the multiple dimensions of realistic integrated solutions to the region's water challenges: ecological, economic, historical, institutional, legal, political, scientific, and technical.

WATERKEEPER

http://waterkeeper.org
Founded by Robert F. Kennedy Jr., Waterkeeper serves as an umbrella to two hundred local Waterkeeper organizations working worldwide to protect rivers, streams, and coastlines. In this global

movement, on-the-water advocates patrol and protect over 100,000 miles of coastline in North and South America, Europe, Australia, Asia, and Africa. Waterkeepers combine firsthand knowledge of their waterways with an unwavering commitment to the rights of their communities and to the rule of law.

WATER.ORG

http://water.org
Cofounded by Matt Damon and Gary White, Water.org is a non-profit organization that has transformed hundreds of communities in Africa, South Asia, and Central America by providing access to safe water and sanitation. It works with local partners to deliver innovative solutions for long-term success. Its microfinance-based WaterCredit Initiative is pioneering sustainable giving in the sector. The organization is a Skoll Foundation grantee and has digitally savvy tools, including a successful partnership with online game company Zynga titled "One Week for Water," and my.water.org, which allows people to follow a community water project.

THE WILDERNESS SOCIETY

www.wilderness.org
The Wilderness Society's mission is to protect wilderness and inspire Americans to care for our wild places. The Wilderness Society has led the effort to permanently protect as designated wilderness nearly 110 million acres in forty-four states, from rich hardwood forests in the East, stunning deserts in the Southwest, and snowcapped peaks in the Rockies to old-growth forests in the Pacific Northwest and tundra in Alaska.

THE WORLD RESOURCES INSTITUTE

www.wri.org

The World Resources Institute (WRI) is a global environmental think tank that goes beyond research to put ideas into action. It works with governments, companies, and civil society to build solutions to urgent environmental challenges. WRI's transformative ideas protect the earth and promote development because sustainability is essential to meeting human needs and fulfilling human aspirations in the future. WRI spurs progress by providing practical strategies for change and effective tools to implement them. It measures its success in the form of new policies, products, and practices that shift the ways governments work, companies operate, and people act.

THE WORLD'S WATER

www.worldwater.org

Worldwater.org is dedicated to providing information and resources to help protect and preserve freshwater around the globe. A project of the Pacific Institute, this site is a companion to its biennial book, *The World's Water,* and also provides links to a wide range of water resources.

B. ONLINE INFORMATION TOOLS

Atrazine information page from Pesticide Action Network, at www
.panna.org/resources/specific-pesticides/atrazine.

Drinking Water Quality Analysis and Tap Water Database from the
Environmental Working Group, at www.ewg.org/tap-water/
home.

Field Level Operations Watch: interactive tool for monitoring water
and sanitation projects worldwide, from Water for People,
at www.waterforpeople.org/programs/field-level-operations
-watch.html.

Global map of regions suffering water stress: "Water Map Shows
Billions at Risk of 'Water Insecurity,'" *BBC News Science &
Environment*, at www.bbc.co.uk/news/science-environment
-11435522.

"Guide to Safe Drinking Water" from the Environmental Working
Group, at www.ewg.org/files/EWG_safedrinkingwater.pdf.

"Heartbeat of a River," interactive graphic from The Nature Conservancy, at www.nature.org/ourinitiatives/habitats/riverslakes/
explore/rivers-and-lakes-the-heartbeat-of-a-river.xml.

Home Water–Energy–Climate Calculator from Pacific Institute, at
www.wecalc.org.

Interactive database of water polluters: "Find Water Polluters Near
You," from the *New York Times,* at http://projects.nytimes
.com/toxic-waters/polluters.

Interactive water-energy map: "Where water meets watts," from the Institute of Electrical and Electronics Engineers, at http://spectrum.ieee.org/static/watermap.

Lake Mead water level calculator and video: "When will Las Vegas run out of water?" from *Las Vegas Sun* newspaper, at www.lasvegassun.com/news/topics/water/.

Location-based guide to water refill sites: "Refill Your Bottle with Clean Sustainable Water on the Go," from TapIt, at www.tapitwater.com.

"Rivers Are Life," interactive graphic from The Nature Conservancy, at www.nature.org/ourinitiatives/habitats/riverslakes/multimedia/rivers-are-life.xml.

US Drought Monitor map, US Department of Agriculture, at http://drought.unl.edu/dm/monitor.html.

Virtual Water: iPhone app by Raureif that shows the water footprint for consumer products, at http://itunes.apple.com/app/virtual-water/id369876250?mt=8.

Water Footprint Calculator from H_2O Conserve, at www.h2oconserve.org/wc.php.

Water Footprint Calculator from National Geographic, at http://environment.nationalgeographic.com/environment/freshwater/water-footprint-calculator.

C. ONLINE WATER CONSERVATION, PROTECTION, AND ACCESS CAMPAIGNS

Takepart.com/last call is the official website for the social action campaign based on the film *Last Call at the Oasis*. Here is a list of other websites offering tools and other opportunities to take action to help solve the water crisis.

CHANGE.ORG ENVIRONMENT

http://news.change.org/environment
Sign a petition, help a campaign, or create a new campaign for a current water issue.

CHARITY: WATER

www.charitywater.org
Create your own fund-raiser on the site for a specific water issue, or help out on one you support.

ECOCLOUD-SUSTAINABLE SILICON VALLEY

http://ecocloud-sv.com
EcoCloud, a project of Sustainable Silicon Valley in conjunction

with public and private-sector partners, is a virtual space where business leaders and facility managers can work with technology innovators, researchers, and government agencies to make enterprises more sustainable and profitable. Drawing on the latest social networking tools, participants can collaborate, learn, plan, and make valuable connections.

FOOD & WATER WATCH

www.foodandwaterwatch.org/water
Sign petitions and participate in water campaigns.

IBM SMARTER WATER MANAGEMENT

www.ibm.com/smarterplanet/us/en/water_management/ideas
This web campaign gives consumers copious amounts of information and ways to get involved, as well as showcases IBM's involvement in technology-driven water projects.

LEVI'S WATER<LESS

http://store.levi.com/waterless
Levi's revolutionized its manufacturing process and introduced the Water<Less jeans line, which uses an average of 28 percent less and as much as 96 percent less water for some products. The company also created an online campaign for using water wisely.

NATIONAL GEOGRAPHIC FRESHWATER CAMPAIGN

http://environment.nationalgeographic.com/environment/
freshwater/about-freshwater-initiative
The National Geographic Society's freshwater initiative is a multiyear
global effort to inspire and empower individuals and communities
to conserve freshwater and preserve the extraordinary diversity of
life that rivers, lakes, and wetlands sustain.

STORY OF BOTTLED WATER

http://storyofstuff.org/bottledwater
This online campaign and video show how bottled water is made,
what effect it has on the environment, and ways to help the project.

UNICEF TAP PROJECT

www.celebritytap.org
Celebrities donate their tap water to be won in a sweepstakes.
Restaurants charge a dollar for tap water and that dollar goes to
UNICEF.

D. BOOKS FOR
FURTHER LEARNING

Barlow, Maude. *Blue Covenant: The Global Water Crisis and the Coming Battle for the Right to Water.* **New York: New Press, 2009.**

Canadian antiglobalization activist Barlow (also author of *Blue Gold*) calls for a "blue covenant" among nations to define the world's freshwater as a human right and a public trust rather than as a commercial product.

Black, Maggie. *The Atlas of Water, Second Edition: Mapping the World's Most Critical Resource.* **Berkeley: University of California Press, 2009.**

This visual guide to the state of water uses vivid graphics, maps, and charts to explore the complex human interaction with water over time and across the world. It also outlines critical tools for managing water, providing safe access to water, and preserving the future of the world's water supply.

Fishman, Charles. *The Big Thirst: The Secret Life and Turbulent Future of Water.* **New York: Free Press, 2011.**

A journalist's overview of humankind's complex relationship with water, the growing problems we have in marshaling adequate water for our growing needs, and emerging technological and social solutions. Fishman writes, "Many civilizations have been crippled or destroyed by an inability to understand water or manage it. We have a huge advantage over the generations of people who have come before us, because we can understand water and we can use it smartly."

Gleick, Peter H., ed. *The World's Water: The Biennial Report on Freshwater Resources*. Washington, DC: Island Press, 2011.

The most comprehensive and up-to-date source of information and analysis on freshwater resources. The 2011–2012 edition (the seventh in the series) features chapters on water policy, transboundary waters, and the effects of fossil fuel production on water resources, among other timely issues, as well as concise updates on topics including bottled water, the Great Lakes Water Agreement, and the state of the Colorado River.

———. *Bottled and Sold: The Story Behind Our Obsession with Bottled Water*. Washington, DC: Island Press, 2011.

A spirited, knowledgeable defense of public water supplies, the story behind the growth of the bottled water industry, and a critique of bottled water companies and their practices around water extraction, advertising, marketing, and environmental protection. Gleick argues forcefully that sustainable water practices would eliminate the need and demand for bottled water.

Glennon, Robert. *Water Follies: Groundwater Pumping and the Fate of America's Fresh Waters*. Washington, DC: Island Press, 2004.

Law professor Glennon studies the use and abuse of groundwater, the antiquated system of laws that permits it, and calls for a halt to the unregulated and uncontrolled exploitation of our limited water resources.

————. *Unquenchable: America's Water Crisis and What to Do About It.* Washington, DC: Island Press, 2010.

> "Connects the dots between our water woes and climate change, energy, growth, the environment, and agriculture. [Glennon] makes a compelling case that we need to re-think how we use this prized resource and provides a number of thought-provoking solutions. Informative, insightful, and very interesting." —US Senator Mark Udall, Colorado.

Imhoff, Daniel. *Food Fight: The Citizen's Guide to a Food and Farm Bill.* California: Watershed Media, 2007.

> Amid the continuing debate over American agriculture, including its impact on water supplies, *Food Fight* offers a highly informative and visually engaging overview of legislation that literally shapes our food system, our bodies, and our future.

Pearce, Fred. *When the Rivers Run Dry: Water—The Defining Crisis of the Twenty-First Century.* Boston: Beacon Press, 2007.

> A disturbing study of the looming cataclysm affecting many of the world's great rivers, from the Amazon to the Nile, the Congo to the Colorado, by a science journalist and former news editor of *New Scientist*.

Postel, Sandra. *Last Oasis: Facing Water Scarcity.* New York: Norton, 1997.

> In this book from the Worldwatch Institute, Sandra Postel shows how decades of profligacy and mismanagement of the world's water resources are leading to shortages and environmental destruction, and she explains the existing technologies that could be used to enhance the productivity of every available liter of water.

Prud'homme, Alex. *The Ripple Effect: The Fate of Fresh Water in the Twenty-First Century.* **New York: Scribner, 2011.**

A globe-trotting overview of the world's greatest water challenges, from depleted aquifers and polluted streams to global climate change. One of the books that inspired the film *Last Call at the Oasis.*

Quinlan, Joseph P. *The Last Economic Super Power: The Retreat of Globalization, the End of American Dominance, and What We Can Do About It.* **New York: McGraw-Hill, 2011.**

This riveting book provides a decidedly broader scope, offering an actionable plan for keeping the United States' seat at the table by avoiding "me-first" isolationism and promoting worldwide economic growth.

Reisner, Mark. *Cadillac Desert: The American West and Its Disappearing Water,* **rev. ed. New York: Penguin, 1993.**

A classic work of history and investigative journalism that tells the story of conflicts over water policy in the West and the resulting damage to the land, wildlife, and Indians. *Publishers Weekly* said this "timely and important book should be required reading for all citizens."

Shiva, Vandana. *Water Wars: Privatization, Pollution, and Profit.* **Cambridge, MA: South End Press, 2002.**

While drought and desertification intensify around the world, corporations are aggressively converting free-flowing water into bottled profits. Vandana Shiva, dubbed by *The Guardian* "the world's most prominent radical scientist," uses the international water trade and industrial activities such as damming, mining, and aquafarming to expose the destruction of the earth and the disenfranchisement of the world's poor as they are stripped of rights to a precious common good.

Solomon, Steven. *Water: The Epic Struggle for Wealth, Power, and Civilization.* **New York: Harper Perennial, 2011.**

> A journalist's narrative account of the water-based power struggles, personalities, and breakthroughs that have shaped humanity from antiquity's earliest civilizations through the steam-powered Industrial Revolution and our dawning age of water scarcity.

E. ABOUT THE DISTRIBUTORS OF
LAST CALL AT THE OASIS

ATO PICTURES

ATO Pictures is the distributor of the film *Last Call at the Oasis*. ATO Pictures, in conjunction with its founder, Dave Matthews of the Dave Matthews Band, and Red Light Management, has a long-standing commitment to environmental causes. In 2011 Dave Matthews partnered with the Brita FilterForGood Music Project, a program that promotes the small steps people can take to make a big difference. Brita and the Dave Matthews Band partnered to help decrease their tour's environmental footprint by reducing bottled water waste with Brita filtered water and reusable Nalgene bottles. By providing concert venues with hydration stations and reusable bottles, Brita helps music fans do their part to promote positive change for the planet. Check out the Brita FilterForGood Music Project on Facebook.

www.atopictures.com
www.redlightmanagement.com
www.filterforgood.com

INDEX

I believe that a good story well told can truly make a difference in how one sees the world. This is why I started Participant Media: to tell compelling, entertaining stories that create awareness of the real issues that shape our lives.

At Participant, we seek to entertain our audiences first and then invite them to participate in making a difference. With each film, we create social action and advocacy programs that highlight the issues that resonate in the film and provide ways to transform the impact of the media experience into individual and community action.

Thirty-six films later, from *An Inconvenient Truth* to *Food, Inc.*, and from *Waiting for "Superman"* to *Contagion* and *The Help*, and through thousands of social action activities, Participant continues to create entertainment that inspires and compels social change. Now through our partnership with PublicAffairs, we are extending our mission so that more of you can join us in making our world a better place.

Jeff Skoll, founder and chairman
Participant Media

PublicAffairs is a publishing house founded in 1997. It is a tribute to the standards, values, and flair of three persons who have served as mentors to countless reporters, writers, editors, and book people of all kinds, including me.

I. F. STONE, proprietor of *I. F. Stone's Weekly*, combined a commitment to the First Amendment with entrepreneurial zeal and reporting skill and became one of the great independent journalists in American history. At the age of eighty, Izzy published *The Trial of Socrates*, which was a national bestseller. He wrote the book after he taught himself ancient Greek.

BENJAMIN C. BRADLEE was for nearly thirty years the charismatic editorial leader of *The Washington Post*. It was Ben who gave the *Post* the range and courage to pursue such historic issues as Watergate. He supported his reporters with a tenacity that made them fearless and it is no accident that so many became authors of influential, best-selling books.

ROBERT L. BERNSTEIN, the chief executive of Random House for more than a quarter century, guided one of the nation's premier publishing houses. Bob was personally responsible for many books of political dissent and argument that challenged tyranny around the globe. He is also the founder and longtime chair of Human Rights Watch, one of the most respected human rights organizations in the world.

•   •   •

For fifty years, the banner of Public Affairs Press was carried by its owner Morris B. Schnapper, who published Gandhi, Nasser, Toynbee, Truman, and about 1,500 other authors. In 1983, Schnapper was described by *The Washington Post* as "a redoubtable gadfly." His legacy will endure in the books to come.

Peter Osnos, *Founder and Editor-at-Large*